Islam Under The Microscope

A Condensed Digest for Muslims
and Non-Muslims

ISLAM UNDER THE MICROSCOPE

A Condensed Digest for Muslims and Non-Muslims

FIROZ-UL HAQUE

ATLANTIC
PUBLISHERS & DISTRIBUTORS (P) LTD

Published by

ATLANTIC

PUBLISHERS & DISTRIBUTORS (P) LTD

B-2, Vishal Enclave, Opp. Rajouri Garden,
New Delhi-110027
Phones : 25413460, 25429987, 25466842

Sales Office
7/22, Ansari Road, Darya Ganj,
New Delhi-110002
Phones : 23273880, 23275880, 23280451
Fax : 91-11-23285873
web : www.atlanticbooks.com
e-mail : info@atlanticbooks.com

ISBN 81-269-0700-2

Printed in India
at Nice Printing Press, Delhi

Dedication

This book is dedicated to my wife, Shaheen, whose conviction to excel and succeed in difficult circumstances, and uphold strong Islamic values, in spite of being educated in catholic parochial institutions, has provided me the strength and motivation to write this book.

Acknowledgements

I am deeply indebted to the support of my daughter Shireen whose constant encouragement was a very important factor. I am also grateful to the management of Al-Hidaya Mosque in Marietta, Georgia, who provided copies of Quran and Sahih Bukhari. Computer support from Cindy Wilson and Tyrone Williams was also a valuable asset. Illustrations by Gerrell Williams, and editing as well as formatting by Kimeri Swift were vital for the success of this book. I am also grateful to various authors and publishers, especially Ms. Ann Moore of *Time Magazine,* and Ms. Tehseen Ahmed of ATP for allowing me to include previously published material in my book.

Firoz-ul Haque

Preface

The greatness of Islam has been presented to the world by a number of scholars, both Muslims and non-Muslims. Some non-Muslim thinkers have embraced Islam because of its openness, flexibility and solid moral values. Sadly speaking, however, a large number of Muslims today have deviated from following Islam in their daily life. Muslims, all over the world, have transformed Islam into a religion of convenience and whims. It is followed to suit personal agenda, and ignored when individual motives clash with Islamic provisions.

Although it is not my intent to write a book on the history of Islam, any book on Islam will be incomplete without historical references. Only through a clear understanding of Islamic history, a reader can differentiate between fact and fiction. It would suffice to say that Islam is neither a mythology nor a fiction. It is a way of life that has been prescribed by Prophet Abraham (pbuh) and his descendant, Muhammad (pbuh) the last prophet.

As a practising Muslim, when I look back and analyze the state of affairs among the Muslims, it saddens me enormously to see that their compromising attitude towards non-Islamic practices is tarnishing the image of this great religion. It is, of course, not my desire to condemn all Muslims because there are many devoted men and women who continue to pursue a true Islamic way of life as prescribed in the Quran* and the Sunna (also written as Sunnah) [(practices of prophet Muhammad (pbuh)]. But many Muslims today are engaged in defaming Islam, partly because of lack of knowledge, and partly due to political and economic reasons. In so doing, they are weakening the foundation and pillars of Islam.

---

* Quran is also written as Qur-an, Qur'an, Koran, etc.

By writing this book, my goal is to reach both Muslims and non-Muslims. It is hoped that Muslims will be able to look at their pitfalls, and get back on the right path. Non-Muslims, on the other hand, are expected to get a clear understanding of Islam which will inculcate them with a sense of respect for Islam, and lead to peaceful coexistence with Muslims, especially in countries where religious strife is a daily occurrence.

This book addresses major issues only and avoids petty issues which are of very little significance, especially to a non-Muslim reader. Although in some primitive societies, petty issues have led to bloodshed, only education and Islamic teaching will eradicate petty differences.

The readers will find frequent references from Quran and Ahadith [reports on the approach of handling life's issues by Prophet Muhammad (pbuh), collectively known as Sunna or Sharia]. As I am not a scholar of the Arabic language, I have solely relied on English translations of Quran by Muhammad Farooq-I-Azam Malik, Dr. Muhammad Taqi-ud-Din Al-Hilali and Dr. Muhammad Muhsin Khan (May the Almighty God shower His blessings on these scholars for their extraordinary work!). I have also depended on the English translation of Ahadith (Sahih Al-Bukhari) by Dr. Muhammad Muhsin Khan. Without these translations, this book could not have been written.

Readers should also understand that the Muslim ummah (community) is plagued with a number of issues or notions. I have attempted to address many issues and their Islamic resolutions. Nevertheless, it is almost impossible to condense all aspects of Islam that are documented in over half a million books and countless internet articles. Only issues that are of global nature have been addressed in this book.

As in any religion, interpretation of provisions varies from scholar to scholar. I have intentionally kept opinions and explanations of Muslim scholars to the minimum, simply because any literate Muslim or non-Muslim is capable of understanding the provisions of Quran and the Ahadith, which are neither complicated nor require undue scholarly briefings.

It is hoped that readers of all walks of life, young and old, Muslims and non-Muslims, will be able to gain a clear understanding of Islam and convey the message of Islam to others. In so doing, they will sow the seed for global peace and non-violence.

Lastly, let it be known that it is not my intent to create a literary, journalistic or historical marvel. I have only attempted to reach the masses, conveying the true message of Islam to both Muslims and non-Muslims, in a style that is easily comprehensible.

Firoz-ul Haque

Contents

List of Illustrations

Introduction to Islam

1

UNDERSTANDING ISLAM

Islam bashing by western historians, and talk show hosts in the United States and elsewhere, especially after the events of September 11, 2001, has become a favorite ratings gathering phenomenon. Negative image of Muslims and Islam is being portrayed by clergy, politicians and average citizens alike. A rush to judgment has become the normal response in the events of a crisis. The entire Muslim ummah is found to be guilty when a terrorist organization such as Al-Qaeda hits a western target.

The general population tends to forget that majority of Muslims in the United States, other G-8 countries, India, and elsewhere, are making enormous contributions in all areas. They are doctors, lawyers, businessmen, professors, teachers, politicians, bankers, and so on. This state is partly due to lack of understanding of Islam, and partly because Muslims have not come forward to explain what Islam is, and what a Muslim is obligated to do.

Among westerners, it is a common belief that expansion of Islam outside Saudi Arabia was possible mainly by Prophet Muhammad's (pbuh) policy of force and coercion.

In the *Decline and Fall of Roman Empire,* Edward Gibbon writes:

> Muhammad, with the sword in one hand and Koran in the other erected his throne on the ruins of Christianity and Rome.

He goes on with his Islam bashing and states:

> In the cave of Hera, three miles from Mecca, he (Muhammad) consulted the spirit of fraud or enthusiasm, whose abode is not in the heavens, but in the mind of the prophet. The faith which under the name Islam, he preached to his family and nation is compounded of an eternal truth and a necessary fiction.

Ironically, Gibbon's high place in history is tainted with ignorance. A rebuttal of such bias is hardly worth wasting one's time. What is important is the diffusion of anti-Islam rhetoric on airwaves by talk show hosts and their guests in the United States and elsewhere. Opinions and comments expressed on the airwave sink into the minds of the general population, which hardly has the time or the zeal to look deeper into this subject and vindicate Islam. They tend to believe what they hear.

The sad event of September 11 has manifested the passage of the PATRIOT ACT by the US government. This act has drastically curtailed the civil rights of all Americans, Muslims and non-Muslims. Due to the "Got You" nature of this act, Muslims are scared to speak up, donate funds to run their schools and mosques, attend their Friday prayers, and travel without fear of persecution. To add fuel to the fire, the political pundits and misinformed journalists have labeled all Madarsas (Islamic Schools) and all mosques as breeding grounds for terrorism.

Edward Gibbon's animosity with Islam has, certainly, been toned down by impartial historians such as Karen Armstrong of Great Britain. She has written one of the most unbiased books on the history of Islam. Mother Armstrong, a catholic nun, in her book *Islam* writes:

> Muhammad had not come to cancel the older religions, to contradict their prophet, or to start a new faith. His message is the same as those of Moses, David, Solomon, and Jesus.

History and historians are known to be both benevolent and cruel. Their views are reflections of the era in which they live and the readership they attempt to impress. Opposing views about Islam or any other subject are important as they offer an opportunity to analyze the subject beyond a superficial level. Only then, an unbiased opinion can be formulated.

As for the expansion of Islam, one needs to look at the depth of Quranic verses, which solidify Islam's non-coercive and non-violent approach to Dawa (conveyance of the message of Islam).

Quran says:

> There is no compulsion in religion. (2:256)
> There is no God but Him. (2:255)
> Do not argue with the People of the Book—and say: we believe in that which is sent down to us and that which is sent down to you. Our God and your God is the same One God. (29:46)

When one analyzes the above Quranic verses, a myriad of thoughts comes to mind, eventually leading to conclusions that make sense to all segments of our society.

These conclusions are:

- Islamic Jurisprudence does not permit conversion to Islam by coercion and force. Any past or present practice by Muslims, contrary to this belief, is not condoned by Islam.
- Islam fosters the belief in one God, which is the same belief fostered by Abraham (pbuh), Moses (pbuh), Jesus (pbuh), and other prophets before Muhammad (pbuh). What differs is the canonical approach discussed later.
- Quran admonishes Muslims to respect the People of the Book (Christians and Jews), as Muhammad (pbuh) had no intentions of introducing a brand new religious philosophy.
- As a respect for Christians and Jews, he even directed the Muslims to face Jerusalem during prayers in the early stages of Islam.

Non-Muslim researchers, and borderline confused Muslims, have often posed the question, "why Islam"? Were Judaism and Christianity not adequate to guide the mankind? One would find the answers of such questions by looking into the history of the Arabian peninsula at the time of the Prophet (pbuh). Paganism had clouded both Christian and Judaic theologies, and Arabs were engaged in anti-Christian and anti-Judaic practices. Their individual and social life was marred with violence, infanticide, polygamy, and various other sociological ills. Furthermore, Muhammad (pbuh) believed that the original message of "Unity of God" had gone through various iterations and alterations over the centuries. These iterations and alterations were deemed responsible for the sociological chaos and the spiritual vacuum of the pagan Arabs. It was because of this chaos and lack of spiritualism that Muhammad the Prophet (pbuh), the great sociologist, and the great thinker introduced the religion of Islam.

The expansion of Islam resulting in approximately 1.2 billion Muslims worldwide cannot be attributed to coercion and violence. It is the fruit of the Islamic values which the Prophet (pbuh) and his true followers propagated and inculcated among communities as far east as Indonesia and as far west as North America.

Muhammad's (pbuh) lineage goes back to Ismael (Ismail), the second son of Abraham (pbuh) from his second wife (or concubine as some historians have reported) Hagar. Abraham abandoned both Hagar and Ismael due to traditions that prevailed at that time. They settled in Mecca and became the forefathers of the Quraish, a well respected tribe to which Muhammad (pbuh) belonged. Ismael too was destined to become the father of a great nation according to the Book of Genesis, 16, 18:18 – 20.* This great nation is Islam.

As stated earlier, Muhammad was simply reinstating the belief of his forefathers and this belief was Islam. Several verses from the Quran authenticate his message and are shown below:

Prayer of Abraham (Ibrahim) and Ismael (Ismail)

Quran says:

O Rabb (Lord), make us both Muslims (submissive to You); and make our descendants a nation that will be Muslims (submissive to You). (2:128)

O Rabb (Lord), appoint from among them a Rasool (messenger) who shall recite to them Your Revelations and teach them the

* *Islam* by Karen Armstrong.

Book and the Wisdom and sanctify them. Surely, You are the All-Mighty, the Wise. (2:129)

Islam—The Religion of Abraham (Ibrahim)

Quran says:

Who but a foolish man will renounce the religion of Ibrahim?—

When his Rabb asked him: "Be a Muslim," he answered, I have become a Muslim to the Rabb (Lord) of the worlds. This was the legacy that Ibrahim left to his sons. (2:130-131)

And this was enjoined by Ibrahim upon his sons and by Ya'qub (Jacob).

"O my sons! Allah has chosen for you the religion, then die not except in the faith of Islam. (2:132)

Note: This implies the submission.

And as for those who believe (in the oneness of Allah) and do righteous good deeds, Allah will pay them their reward in full. And Allah does not like the Zaliman (polytheists and wrong doers). (3:57)

Say: O People of the Scripture (Jews and Christians): come to a word that is just between us and you, that we worship none but Allah (alone) and that we associate no partners with Him and that none of us shall take others as Lords besides Allah. (3:64)

Say: Truly, my Lord has guided me to a straight path, a right religion, and the religion of Ibrahim, Hanifa (true Islamic monotheism). (6:161)

Note: "say" here is addressing the Prophet (pbuh).

Say (O Muhammad) verily, my salat (prayers), my sacrifice, my living, and my dying are for Allah, the Lord of the Worlds. (6:162)

The true meaning of Islam seems to have been grossly misinterpreted by western news media. It is, therefore, crucial that readers understand what Islam stands for. It is hoped that the current practice of "rush-to-judgment" and "conviction without a trial" will be alleviated when readers develop an understanding of Islam. Only credible information and education will minimize, if not eradicate, the distrust of Muslims and a dislike for Islam. The burden of educating adversaries and foes of Islam lies upon Muslims who seem to have taken a back seat.

MEANING OF ISLAM

"Islam" is an Arabic word, which has two meanings:

1. Submission and Obedience
2. Peace

The religious connotation of Islam is total submission and obedience to God (Allah). Only through this submission, one can achieve complete peace of mind and heart.

Islam fosters creation of a just society in which all members, rich or poor, ruler or subject, black or white, weak or strong, male or female, are treated with respect and compassion. Any behavior pattern or practice contrary to this belief is not encouraged by Islam.

PROPHETHOOD OF MUHAMMAD (pbuh)

The evolution of Quran is the greatest testimony of the prophethood of Muhammad (pbuh). The prophethood of Muhammad (pbuh) is also written in the Bible (Duet 18:18, 18:15, 33:23; Isaiah 29:12; Songs of Solomon 5:16 and John 14:15-16).*

It is, however, important to emphasize that Muhammad (pbuh) was a human being who was chosen by God to convey His (God's) message to his people. He resisted every effort to glamorize himself. Quran is very explicit about this.

Quran says:

> Say: "I do not claim that I possess the treasures of Allah or that—I know the unseen nor do I claim that I am an angel. What I say is that I follow only that which is revealed to me. (6:50)
>
> He alone has the keys of the unseen treasures, of which no one knows except Him. He knows whatever is in the land and in the sea; there is not a single leaf that falls without His knowledge. (6:59)

Note: He, Him, and His herein stand for Allah (God).

---

* *Muhammad in Bible* by Dr. J. Badawi, published by IBS in co-operation with Al-Sunnah. Com, Kuwait.

EXPANSION OF ISLAM

Expansion of Islam in the prophet's lifetime is credited to his dual role—a messenger of God and a masterful statesman. Even his enemies were convinced that his jurisprudence was extraordinarily brilliant. He continued to lead a simple life, milked his own goat, and was accessible to his ummah day or night. His administration was a blend of justice and mercy. He was gentle and merciful even to his enemies. As one biographer writes:

> In the gift of influencing men he (Muhammad) had the nobility to influence them for good.*

Edward Gibbon's "Expansion of Islam by Sword" theory has been proven to be inaccurate by numerous non-Muslim scholars and thinkers. A few excerpts from various publications compiled by The Institute of Islamic Information and Education (IIIE) are presented here to enlighten the uninformed readers.

MAHATMA GANDHI (a Hindu politician and champion of non-violence)

"I became more and more than ever convinced that it was not the sword that won Islam a place for Islam in those days in scheme of life. It was the rigid simplicity, the utter self-effacement of the prophet, the scrupulous regard for his pledges, his intense devotion to his friends and followers, his intrepidity, his

* *Man's Religions* by John Boyer Noss, published by MacMillan Publishing, New York.

fearlessness, his absolute trust in God, and his mission" (published in *Young India*, 1924).

YUSUF ISLAM (Cat Stevens, world famous British pop singer)

"It will be wrong to judge Islam in the light of the behavior of some bad Muslims who are always shown on the media. It is like judging a car as a bad one if the driver of the car is drunk, and he bangs it into a wall. Islam guides all human beings in daily life—in its spiritual, mental, and physical dimensions. But we must find the sources of these instructions, Quran and the examples of the Prophet (pbuh). Then we can see the ideals of Islam."

MUHAMMAD ALI (Cassius Clay, former world heavy weight boxing champion)

"It was an exhilarating experience to see people belonging to different colors, races, nationalities, kings, heads of states, and ordinary men from very poor countries, all clad in two simple white sheets praying to God without any sense of either pride or inferiority. It was a practical manifestation of the concept of equality in Islam" (Embraced Islam in 1965).

WILFRIED HOFFMAN, Ph.D. (Harvard) (German Social Scientist and Diplomat)

"Islam, undoubtedly, finds itself in the greatest harmony with over all reality" (Embraced Islam in 1980).

BOGDAN KOPANSKI, Ph.D. (Polish American historian)

"I saw a typical example of rebel generation of Reds. In 1974, I visited Turkey, I wrote my MA dissertation. There I was hit by the most beautiful voice of mankind ADHAN, the call to prayer. My hair stood up. Unknown powerful force led me to old masjid in Istanbul. I confessed to tears SHAHADAH, prayed my first SALAH.

I swept out the rubbish ideologies. The first time in my life, my mind was relaxed and I felt pleasure of Allah's love in my heart. I was a Muslim."

These are only a few examples from the work compiled by IIIE (May Allah the Almighty reward them for their good work!). Numerous other testimonies are in existence that negate Gibbon's accounts. One noteworthy attestation is that of Malcolm X.

MALCOLM X

During his pilgrimage to Mecca he wrote to Alex Haley and to an assistant:

> I think I'm the first American born Negro to make the actual Hajj.
>
> I have been utterly speechless and spellbound by the graciousness
>
> I see displayed all around me by the people of all colors.*

* *Speaking Freely, A Memoir* by Nat Henthoff, published by Alfred A. Knopf, Inc.

The greatness of Islam can be summarized with the following verse from Quran:

Quran says:

> Call people to the way of your Rabb with wisdom and best advice, and reason with them, if you have to, in the most courteous manner—the best reward indeed is for those who endure with patience. (16:125-126)

Muhammad (pbuh) had the foresight to understand that for a community to achieve salvation and eternal peace, the community must follow certain guidelines. He introduced the Muslims to the five pillars of Islam and the six articles of faith. Muslims, men and women, are expected to abide by them and make them a part of their daily life.

CANONICAL ASPECTS OF ISLAM

PILLARS OF ISLAM

1. Declaration of one God (SHAHADA)

This is the cornerstone of Islam...to be a Muslim one must believe in "There is no God worthy of worship but Allah, and Muhammad (pbuh) is his messenger." It is the acceptance or rejection of this belief that differentiates a Muslim from a non-Muslim.

2. Prayers (SALAT)

Daily prayers are mandatory. A Muslim must pray five times a day facing the Kaba (pronounced as Kaa-Ba). Prayers are performed at dawn, noon, afternoon, sunset, and night fall. Prayers can be performed anywhere, though congregation in a mosque is desirable. This gives a Muslim man and woman an opportunity to socialize and discuss common issues. During prayers all Muslims, rich or poor, black or white, ruler or subject, stand together to pray. This symbolizes equality of mankind in Islam and discourages segregation as well as division based on color, creed, national origin, and social status. While Sunni Muslims are particular about five distinct prayer times, Shia Muslims, normally, combine the five prayers into three prayers.

3. Fasting (SAUM)

In the month of Ramadan, the ninth month of the lunar calendar, Muslims all over the world observe fasting. A Muslim, while fasting, refrains from eating, drinking, smoking, sex, profanity, and temper outburst.

Aside from helping to maintain a healthy life by resting the body, and losing weight, fasting inculcates a sense of patience, discipline, self-restraint, will power, and awareness of the needs of the hungry and the destitute.

4. Charity (ZAKAT)

Every Muslim whose net annual savings are above a specified minimum, must pay 2.5 per cent of this saving to the poor and the needy. The benefit of Zakat is purification of wealth, eradication of greed and selfishness, reduction of resentment and envy between rich and poor, and development of feelings of sacrifice for others.

5. Pilgrimage to Mecca (HAJJ)

Hajj is an act of worship that a Muslim must perform once in his lifetime if financially and physically capable. Hajj is performed in Mecca, Saudi Arabia, where around two million Muslims, men and women, from all over the world gather to submit to the call of Allah. Hajj creates and reinforces the belief that all Muslims are equal irrespective of their geographical, cultural, and racial origins.

ARTICLES OF FAITH

1. A Muslim believes in one God "Allah", and Allah alone must be worshipped (monotheism).
2. A Muslim believes in all messengers of Allah, beginning with Adam (pbuh) and ending with Muhammad (pbuh).
3. A Muslim believes in all scriptures of Allah in their original form. In Quran, a special reference is made to the Suhuf (the books of Abraham), the Torah (the book of Moses), the Zabur (the book of David), and the Injeel (the Gospel of Jesus). These revealed books were either lost or altered long before Muhammad (pbuh) was born.

Because of this Allah revealed Quran to the Prophet (pbuh) to be the final revelation and guidance for all mankind.

4. A Muslim believes in the existence of angels.
5. A Muslim believes in the Day of Judgment and an eternal life after death. The quality of this eternal life will depend upon the good and bad deeds performed on this earth, good deeds leading to the Heaven and bad deeds leading to the Hell.
6. A Muslim believes that the destiny of a man or a woman is predetermined by Allah.

It would suffice to say at this point that there are numerous scholarly publications available on this subject to expand one's knowledge of Islam.

MAJOR BRANCHES OF ISLAM

Any book on Islam will be incomplete without getting acquainted with the branches of Islam that emerged after the death of the Prophet Mohammad. The foundation for the various branches was the sectarian and ideological differences that surfaced in absence of the Prophet (pbuh). According to an internet article published in Real-Islam.Org, there are seventy-three branches within Islam, as shown in Appendix A. In addition, the Nation of Islam, the creed that originated in the United States, and serves the spiritual needs of a segment of the black population, is also discussed herein. The readers should note that many of the seventy-three branches within Islam, as well as the Nation of Islam, are considered as non-Muslims by most Sunnis and Shias.

The division in Islam was purely political in nature and had little to do with Islam. After the death of the Prophet, the Muslim ummah was governed by a chosen leader called Khalifa (Caliph). The first three caliphs were Abu Bakar, Umar and Uthman. Dissension among Muslims started in or around 656 A.D. when disgruntled Muslim soldiers emphatically wanted Ali, the prophet's son-in-law, to be the caliph.

Their perception was that the Prophet (pbuh) wanted him (Ali) to be the next caliph. Muslim ummah was, subsequently, split and constituted what is Sunni and Shia today. Sunnis, the segment of Muslims who faithfully observed the Sunnah (Practices of the Prophet) disagreed with Ali's ascension to caliphhood. Dissension of Ali's supporters was somewhat strengthened by Ali's disagreement with the methodologies of Abu Bakar and Umar. This disagreement and Ali's hands off attitude further deepened the rift among their followers. This rift is quite vivid today in all Muslim countries. Periodic clashes between the two sects have taken many lives. The question one must ask "Do Islamic teachings propagate these clashes?" The answer, of course, is NO. It is simply a matter of "who controls who" and "who controls what." The seven-year war between Iraq and Iran, invasion of Kuwait by Iraq, rise of insurgency and suicide bombing in Iraq caused by the loss of Sunni power base, tribal fighting in Afghanistan, ruthless killing of the members of the Shia and Qadiani sects in Pakistan by Sunni extremists, and the massacre of innocent Diwali (a festival of lights) shoppers in India, are testimonies of disregard for Islam in favor of a personal, communal, and tribal agenda.

Sadly enough, the Shias today have forgotten that Ali, in spite of his differences, continued the tradition of Muhammad (pbuh). He emphasized the importance of justice and compassion. He never forgot the Prophet's mission of promoting unity among the Muslims and integrating the ummah. Even when he was deposed by Muawiya, he accepted to step down from the caliphhood rather than confront him with force, thus preventing bloodshed among the ummah. The message here for Sunnis is to evaluate their anti-Shia practices. If they claim to be protectors of the Prophet's traditions, they must adhere to his message and carry out his mission of unity among Muslims.

Quran says:

> All together hold fast to the rope of Allah and be not divided among yourselves. Remember Allah's favor upon you when you were enemies;
>
> He united your hearts, so by His favor you became brethren. (3:103)

Be not like those who became divided into sects and who started to argue against each other after clear revelations had come to them.

THOSE RESPONSIBLE FOR DIVISION AND

ARGUMENTS WILL BE STERNLY PUNISHED. (3:105)

Quran and Ahadith are sources of knowledge for both Sunnis and Shias. It is simply a matter of interpretation and not the contents of the sources.

BRANCHES OF ISLAM

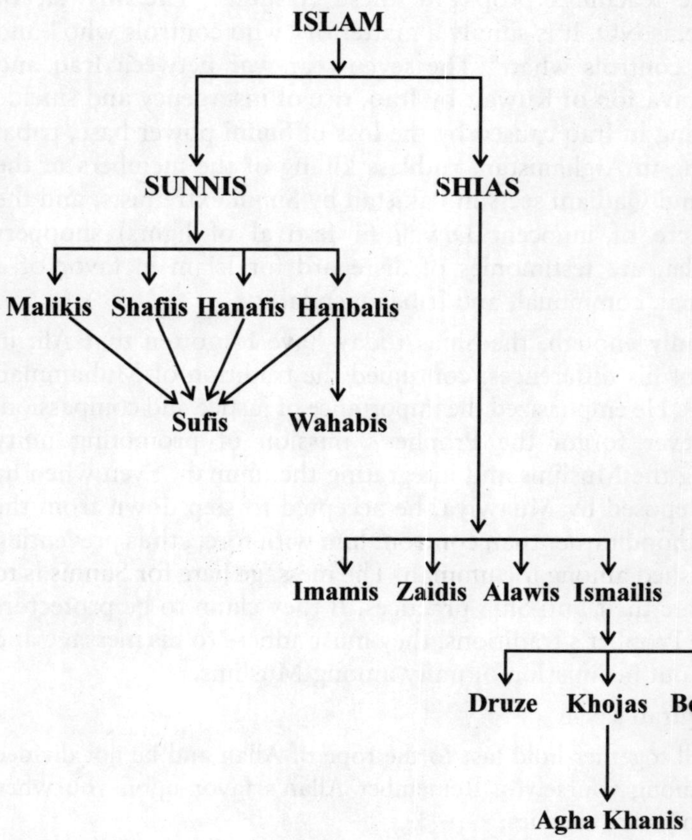

THE SUNNI MADHHAB (or MAZHAB)

Four major madhhabs evolved after the death of the Prophet (pbuh). These Madhhabs were based on the interpretations of the Prophet's (pbuh) message, practices, and the way of life. Readers must, however, understand that these interpretations are simply guidelines to achieve the same goal that the Prophet (pbuh) had conveyed to the Muslim ummah: "total submission and obedience to Allah." Details of the history of these Madhhabs can be found in many books on the history of Islam. A brief description of these Madhhabs is presented here for the benefit of the readers. These four Madhhabs were dominant in different parts of the world—Maliki doctrine in north and central Africa, Shafii law in Egypt and southern Arabia, Hanafi system in western Asia, and the Hanbali practices in Saudi Arabia and the Indian sub-continent only after the beginning of the Wahabi reform in the eighteenth century.

These four Madhhabs are intertwined in the fabric of Sunni doctrine and do not differ markedly from one another.

Maliki Madhhab

The Maliki madhhab was championed by Malik-ibn-Anas. Malikis were the most conservative of the four madhhabs and continued the consensus of Medina, which was the center of Islamic activities during and after the Prophet's (pbuh) time. They had a more moralistic view in which the intentions of a person, good or bad, were taken into account in determining their permissibility.

Shafii Madhhab

Al-Shafii, the promoter of the Shafii madhhab, was a student of Imam Malik whose teachings had a profound effect on Shafii. He, nevertheless, stressed on FIQH (pronounced as fik similar to fig, and means jurisprudence) and emphasized four roots of sacred law—the Quran, the Sunnah, the Qias (analogy), and the Ijmah (consensus). Sunnis in Shafii's time were divided into two schools. The Ahl-al-kalam (the rationalists) who defended the supremacy of Quran, and the Ahl-al-hadith (traditionalists or the People of the Book) for whom the Prophet's example was most important. Shafii successfully merged these two schools and created a unified system called Sharia or Divine Law of Islam.

Hanafi Madhhab

The chief architect of the Hanafi madhhab was Abu Hanifa, a Murijite. He also put emphasis on fiqh and stressed on a man's interior judgment. Abu Hanifa had realized that the Quran contained very little legislation, and the laws therein, were designed for a much simpler society. He and his disciples embarked upon a quest for collecting Ahadith (reports on the prophet's and his companion's approach of handling life's issues). This quest paid off and Abu Hanifa became the greatest legal expert. Although he wrote very little himself, his disciples preserved his teachings. The most widely used Ahadith today are compiled by al-Bukhari and Muslim. But there are other collections as well which can be found in Islamic book stores and libraries.

Hanbali Madhhab

The Hanbali madhhab was pioneered by Ahmad-ibn-Hanbal. His doctrine stressed on realistic or non-allegorical interpretation of Quran. Nevertheless, the Hanbalis always remained an opposition group within the wider Islamic culture. They failed to constitute a school of fiqh comparable to the other three madhhabs.

REFORMS IN THE SUNNI MADHHAB

SUFISM

Sufis, followers of Sufism, were pious Muslims who believed that through meditation and self-discipline, they could attain a direct personal experience of God. They developed an approach to Islam based on personal piety. Through Sufism, Islam was able to absorb the traditions of other religions that may have been non-Islamic in nature but were deeply rooted in the culture of people converted to Islam.

Sufis were the most effective missionaries. Through their efforts, Islam reached far corners of the globe. Often, it is misunderstood that Sufis endured mystic experiences and had healing power. Even today, their followers flock to their tombs (Mazars) and ask for the fulfilment of individual wishes (a practice not condoned by Quran and Sharia). In reality, Sufis strengthened the Sharia and strongly adhered to it. Their primary goal was to guide the Muslim ummah and steer them in the direction of the original Islam while maintaining their local traditions. Although paying respect and homage to Sufis is acceptable, the practice of tomb worship is not.

WAHABISM

Since the arrest of a Wahabi Chaplain, Captain James Yee (a West Point graduate and converted Muslim), assigned to offer Islamic services to the Talibans in Guantanamo Bay, the words Wahabi and Wahabism have become well-known in the United States and elsewhere. News media and talk show hosts, as usual, were quick to convict him for treason, a charge that has been dropped and Captain Yee has resigned his commission and been honorably discharged.

Wahabism is credited to Muhammad-ibn-Abdal Wahab, an ideologist and co-founder of the Saudi state along with King Abdul Aziz. Wahabism allows any thing not explicitly forbidden in Quran or the Sunnah bypassing the superstructure of fiqh (jurisprudence). IT IS A REFORM IN ISLAM BASED ON A STRICTLY LITERAL INTERPRETATION OF QURAN AND THE SUNNAH. It is practiced mainly in Saudi Arabia, Syria, and the Indian sub-continent. An emergence of Wahabism in the United States, Canada, and the European countries is credited to Muslim immigrants.

Common prohibitions in Wahabism are tomb worship as practiced in India, Pakistan, Iran, and Egypt, music, dancing, poetry, silk, gold jewelry, and tobacco smoking.

It would appear that Abdal Wahab and his followers simply believed in leading a simple and modest life to emulate the lifestyle of the Prophet (pbuh). Nevertheless, some of these prohibitions are neither supported by Quran nor by many scholars.

Quran says:

> As for those who have faith and do good deeds, Allah will certainly admit them to gardens beneath which rivers flow. They shall be decked with PEARLS and bracelets of GOLD and their garments will be of SILK. (22:23)
>
> As for the righteous, they will be in a secure place, among gardens of springs, dressed in fine SILK and rich brocade. (44:53)
>
> Their garments will be of fine green SILK and GOLD embroidery. They will be adorned with bracelet of SILVER. (76:21)

The nine dollar question is (as we say in America)—if the paradise dwellers would have the luxury of silk, gold, silver, and pearl in the next life, what prevents the Muslims from enjoying them in this life? It is certain that some Wahabi scholar has a lot of explaining to do.

With regard to singing and music, Dr. Al-Qaradawi* has very well presented his views on this subject. The bottom line is that "No sound Hadith is available concerning the prohibition of singing. Ibn Hazm, a prominent jurist of Islam, says: 'All that is reported on this subject is false and fabricated.'" The prohibition, according to scholars, is legitimate when singing and music involve drinking of alcohol, obscenity, arousal of passion, and elements that lead to adultery, such as close contact of unmarried male and female as seen in discos, bars, and in both Hollywood and Bollywood movies.

The same logic applies to poetry. Poetry can be very energizing such as the following verses from the poems of the revolutionary Indian poet Dr. Iqbal, who not only boosted the moral, but also mobilized the Indians in their pursuit for gaining independence from the British.

> "The world isn't small for a hard working man, but he must have the heart of a tiger and the zeal to search of an eagle." (Translation from the Urdu language).

---

* *The Lawful and Prohibited in Islam* by Dr. Yusuf Al-Qaradawi, published by American Trust Publications, Burr Ridge, Illinois, USA.

"You are an Eagle; learn to survive on mountain rocks." (translation from Urdu).

Poetry can also be mentally invigorating, such as William Wordsworth's 'Daffodils', and Elizabeth Browning's 'Sonnet from the Portuguese' (see Appendix B for these poems). These poems, even today, inculcate a sense of appreciation for nature and beauty, both attributed to God. Poetry can also be a neuron stimulus and slows down the progression of incurable diseases such as Alzheimer.

Albeit, there is also a brand of poetry which, aside from maintaining the literary stature of a linguistic community, does very little for both Muslims and non-Muslims. This is the form of poetry in which the poet compares the cheeks of his mistress with roses (William Shakespeare's Sonnet 130), the vibrations of the lips of a woman is about to finish the poet (Mirza Ghalib, a contemporary Indian poet), and a myriad of other poems which immortalize Romeo and Juliet, drown a frustrated lover in a pool of alcohol, and compel a poet to express his sentiments about the beauty and physique of a pretty woman he sees on a street corner. Muslim scholars, Wahabis included, are justified in imposing prohibitions against this type of poetry. Nevertheless, poetry as a whole is not an evil that Islam prohibits. Wahabi scholars of our time need to rethink about the various prohibitions and come up with the needed reform.

THE SHIA MADHHAB

As in the Sunni madhhab, after the death of the Prophet (pbuh) and Ali, the first Imam of the Shia sect, four major branches of the Shia madhhab emerged as well. A synopsis of these madhhabs (doctrines) is presented below:

Imamis

Prevalent in Iran, Iraq, Turkey, India, Pakistan, and Persian Gulf states. Imamism is the main branch of the Shia sect and the followers are referred to as TWELVERS because they trace their hierarchy to twelve imams*, beginning with Ali and ending with

* The twelve Imams are: Ali, Hassan, Hussain, Sajjad, Bakar, Sadiq, Moosa-bin-Jafar, Reza, Mohd Naqi, Haadi, Hassan Askari, Mehdi.

the twelfth Imam Mehdi, who by Shia belief, is in hiding and will return one day to purify the world.

Their belief in the hidden Imam has inculcated a sense of tolerance and ability to put up with evils because they are convinced that the twelfth Imam will set the world straight when he returns. Nevertheless, the spiritual leaders today are totally different from the earlier Imams who stayed aloof from politics and refrained from wielding political power. The Ayatollahs of Iran and Iraq are mobilizing the masses, and exercising enormous power over the military, economy, and social structure. From the quietest form of Shiaism, they have transformed twelverism into a vocal, highly traditionalistic, and politically active reformation, often in collision with the rest of the Muslim world.

Zaidis

Zaidism is prevalent in Yemen. The founder of Zaidism was Zaid, a grandson of Hussain (one of the sons of Ali and the second Imam). Zaidis reject the concept of hidden Imam and do not believe in dynastic succession like other Shias do. Zaidis are closer to Sunnis than other branches of Shia Madhhab.

Alawis (Nusairis)

Prevalent in Syria. It is generally believed that Alawis worship Ali as their God. This is in total defiance with original Islam and thus they are considered as non-Muslims. The Alawis, however, claim to be Muslim. This claim was endorsed by a Shia Imam, Musa Sadar of Lebanon for political reasons.*

Alawis developed a Trinitarian doctrine (similar to Christianity) of emanation in the person of Muhammad (pbuh), Ali and Salman-al-Farisi (a companion of the prophet)**. The Alawis trace their lineage back to Ali Naqi, the tenth Imam of the Shia, and believe that their Imam has gone into hiding.

---

* *Faith & Power, The Politics of Islam* by Edward Mortimer, p. 49, a Random House Publication.

** *Islam in the World* by Malise Ruthven, pp. 209-10, published by Oxford University Press.

Ismaelis

Prevalent in the Indian sub-continent and Egypt. Ismaelis believe that Ali's lineage had ended with Ismael, son of Jafar-as-Sadiq, their seventh Imam (spiritual leader) and salvation of mankind would be inaugurated by the seventh prophet Mehdi, who is yet to come [(Adam, Noah, Abraham, Moses, Jesus, and Muhammad were the six great Prophets (may peace be upon them)]. The flip side of the Ismaeli doctrine is the elevation of Ali and their Imam to almost god-like status which is looked at with disgust by all Sunnis and most Shias.*

Nevertheless, Ismaelism offered the more intellectual Muslims a chance to study the new philosophy in a religious way. They, like all true Muslims, inspire for the betterment of the community and believe that faith is worthless unless it is combined with political activism.

Their ideology sets them apart from the mainstream of Islam, and some Sunni Muslims regard them as non-Muslims. It must, however, be noted that majority of scientific and mathematical achievements by Muslims is credited to Ismaelis. Their intellectual superiority has made them successful in both business and academics. The concept of Imam is central to the Ismailis. The role of Imam is to foster group loyalty and guide them to achieve political and social success.

The sub-groups within Ismailism are the Druze, the Khojas (also known as Agha Khanis) and the Bohoras (also known as Mustalis).

The Druze

Prevalent in Lebanon, Syria, and Israel. The Druze revere the divinity of their Imam to a magnitude that takes them outside the core value of true Islam. As in Hinduism and Buddhism, and some Greek mythologies, the Druze believe in the transmigration of soul. The secretive nature of their religion does not allow any converts. Both men and women can be indoctrinated into their secret faith.

---

* *Islam in the World,* p. 206.

The Khojas

Prevalent in India, Pakistan, Syria, Britain, and East Africa. The Khoja community reveres their Imam, Harvard educated Agha Khan who claims to be a descendant of Nizar, a Fatimide, whose lineage goes back to Muhammad's (pbuh) daughter Fatima. They, therefore, call themselves Nizari Ismaelis.

Their Imam, Agha Khan, controls a vast fortune worldwide. His spiritual authority has enabled him to impose religious and legal obligations on his followers. This imposition has enabled the Agha Khanis to become the wealthiest community outside the oil region. This is something that Sunni Muslims have not been able to achieve and are often envious about it.

The Bohras (Mustalis)

Prevalent in India and Pakistan. As all Ismaelis, the Bohoras claim their alliance to the members of ahl-al-bait. They were originally Hindus who converted to Nizari Ismaeli sect of Islam in the eleventh century. They subsequently broke away from Nizari Ismaelism.

The Bohras also have various groups, the largest being the Daudis who pledge their allegiance to their spiritual leader, Sydena Muhammad Burhanuddin. They are the most conservative among all Bohras when it involves Islamic law, but on the other hand, they are progressive enough to accept modern technology and western culture so long as Islamic laws are not violated.

PSEUDO-ISLAMIC SECTS BEFORE THE 21st CENTURY

Aside from the two major branches of Islam, the 20th and 21st centuries have seen various groups wave the banner of Islam. These groups have embraced a pseudo-Islamic theology which contradicts the original Islam. Nevertheless, in spite of their misguided beliefs and anti-Islamic slogans, they deserve the same treatment as the Prophet had given to the members of the minorities. Granted that both Sunni and Shia Muslims consider them as non-Muslims, it is their Islamic duty to co-exist with them peacefully in the same manner as they co-exist with Christians, Jews, and other minorities.

THE NATION OF ISLAM
(Origin in United States)

The original pioneers of the Nation of Islam were Elijah Muhammad and W.D. Fard in the United States. Their approach to Islam was based on racial segregation, a practice hated by Islam. Elijah Muhammad is regarded as the prophet of Allah and W.D. Fard has assumed the role of Allah. After their death, their successor, W.D. Muhammad, became a mainstream Muslim and integrated his community into the original Islam. Subsequently, Louis Farrakhan joined him but broke away and re-started the Nation of Islam. It would suffice to mention that Louis Farrakhan and his followers do not follow the pillars of Islam and the articles of faith. In strict Islamic sense, they can be regarded as non-Muslims.

APPENDIX A

BRANCHES OF ISLAM

(Basic Belief Distinguishing it from Others)

NAME OF THE SECT

JARUDIS. Followers of Abu'l-Jarud. They believe Prophet (pbuh) designated Ali (ra) as the Imam by his characteristics but not by name.

SULAIMANIS/JARIRIS. Followers of Sulaiman ibn-Jarir al-Zaidi. They believed Imamat was a matter of conference and could be confirmed by two best Muslims.

BUTRIS/HURARIS. They did not dispute the Khilafat of Uthman, neither they attack him nor praise him.

YAQUBIS. They accepted the Khilafat of Abu Bakr and Umar, but did not reject those who rejected these Khulafaa. They also believed that Muslim committers of Major sins will be in hellfire forever.

HANAFIS. Followers of the Imamat of Muhammad ibn-al-Hanifah. They believe that Allah might have had a beginning.

KARIBIS. They believed that Imam Muhammad ibn-al-Hanifah is not dead and is the Imam Ghaib (in disappearance) and the expected Mehdi.

KAMILIS. Followers of Abu-Kamil. They believed companions to be heretic because they forsook their allegiance to Ali and condemn Ali for ceasing to fight them. They believed in the returning of the dead before the Day of Resurrection and that Satan is right in preferring fire to clay.

MUHAMMADIS/MUGHAIRIS. Followers of Muhammad ibn-Abdullah ibn-al-Hassan. They do not believe that Imam Muhammad ibn-Abdullah died and that he is Imam Ghaib and awaited Mehdi.

BAQIRIS. Followers of Muhammadibn-Ali al-Baqir. They believe him to be the Imam Ghaib and expected Mehdi.

NADISIS. They believe that those who consider themselves better than anyone else are Kafirs (disbelievers).

SHAIS. They believe that the one who has recited La-Ilaha Il-Allah (There is none worthy of worship except Allah), whatever she or he does, will never be punished.

AMMALIS. They believe that faith for one is what he/she sincerely practices.

ISMAILIS. They believe in the continuity of Imamat among the descendants of Ismail ibn-Ja'far.

MUSAWIS. They believe Musa ibn-Ja'far to be the Imam Ghaib and expected Mehdi.

MUBARIKIS. They believe in the continuity of Imamat among the descendants of Muhammad ibn-Ismail ibn-Ja'far.

KATHIS/ITHNASHARIS. They believe that expected Mehdi will be the twelfth Imam among the descendants of Ali ibn-abi-Talib.

HASHAMIS/TARAQIBIS. They Predicate a body to Allah and also allege Prophet (pbuh) of disobedience to Allah.

ZARARIS. They believed that Allah did not live nor had any attributes till He created for Himself life and His attributes.

YOUNASIS. Followers of Younas ibn-Abd-al-Rahman al-Kummi. They believe that Allah is borne by bearers of His Throne, though He is stronger than them.

SHAITANIS. They believed in the view that deeds of servants of Allah are substances; and a servant of Allah can really produce a substance.

AZRAQIS. Followers of Nafi ibn-al-Azraq. They do not believe in the good dreams and vision and claim that all forms of revelation has ended.

NAJADATS. Followers of Najdah ibn-Amir al-Hanafi. They abolished the punishment for drinking wine also they believed that sinners of this sect would not be treated in hellfire but some other place before allowed in paradise.

SUFRIS. Followers of Ziyad ibn-al-Asfar. They believed that sinners are in fact polytheists.

AJARIDAHS. Followers of Abd-al-Karim ibn-Ajrad. They believed that a child should be called to Islam after it has attained maturity. Also they believed booty of war to be unlawful till the owner is killed.

KHAZIMIS. They believe Allah loves men of all faiths even if one has been disbeliever most of his life.

SHUAIBIS/HUJJATIS. They believe that what Allah desires does happen no matter what and what does not happen it means Allah desires it not.

KHALAFIS. Followers of Khalaf. They do not believe in fighting except under the leadership of an Imam.

MA'LUMIS/MAIHULIS. They believed that whoever did not recognize Allah by all His names was ignorant of Him and anyone ignorant of Him was a disbeliever.

SALTI. Followers of Salt ibn-Uthman. They believed in the conversion of adults only and if father has converted to Islam children were considered disbeliever till they reach maturity.

HAMZIS. Followers of Hamza ibn-Akrak. They believe that children of polytheists are condemned to hell.

THA'LIBIS. Followers of Tha'labah ibn-Mashkan. They believe that parents remain guardian over their children of any age until children make it clear to parents that they are turning away from truth.

MA'BADIS. They did not believe in taking or giving alms from or to slaves.

AKHNASIS. They do not believe in waging a war except in defense or when the opponent is known personally.

SHAIBANIS/MASBBIS. Followers of Shaiban ibn-Salamah al-Khariji. They believe Allah resembles His creatures.

RASHIDIS. They believe that land watered by springs, canals or flowing rivers should pay half the Zakat (Tithe), while land watered by rain only should pay the full Zakat.

MUKARRAMIS/TEHMIS. Followers of Abu-Mukarram. They believe that ignorance constitutes disbelief. Also that Allah's enmity or friendship depends upon the state of a person's belief at his death.

IBADIS. Consider Abdullah ibn-Ibad as their Imam. They believe in doing good deeds without the intention of pleasing Allah.

HAFSIS. Consider Hafs ibn-abi-l-Mikdam as their Imam. They believe that only knowing Allah frees one from polytheism.

HARITHIS. Followers of Harith ibn-Mazid-al-Ibadi. They believe that the ability precedes the deeds.

ASHABTA'AHS. They believe that Allah can send a prophet without giving him any sign to prove his prophecy.

SHABIBIS/SHALIHIS. Followers of Shabib ibn-Yazid al-Shaibani. They believe in the Imamat of a woman named Ghazalah.

WASILIS. Followers of Wasil ibn-Ata al-Ghazza. They believe that those who commit major sins will be punished in hell but still remain believers.

AMRIS. Followers of Amr ibn-Ubaid ibn-Bab. They reject the legal testimony of people from supporters of either side of the battle of Camel.

HUDHAILIS/YAHFANIS. Followers of Abu-al-Hudhail Muhammad ibn-al-Hudhail. They believe that both Hell and Paradise will perish and that preordination of Allah can cease, at which time Allah will no longer be omnipotent.

NAZZAMIS. Followers of Abu-Ishaq Ibrahim ibn-Saiyar. They do not believe in the miraculous nature of the Holy Quran nor do they believe the miracles of Holy Prophet (pbuh) like splitting the moon.

MU'AMMARIS. They believe that Allah neither creates life nor death but it is an act of the nature of living body.

BASHRIS. Followers of Bashr ibn-al-Mu'tamir. They believe that Allah may forgive a man for his sins and may change His mind about this forgiveness and punish him if he is disobedient again.

HISHAMIS. Followers of Hisham ibn-Amr al-Futi. They believe that if a Muslim community come to consensus it need an Imam and if it rebels and kills its Imam, no one should be chosen an Imam during a rebellion.

MURDARIS. Followers of Isa ibn-Sabih. They believe that staying in close communication with the Sultan (ruler) makes one unbeliever.

JA'FRIS. Followers of Ja'far ibn-Harb and Ja'far ibn-Mubashshir. They believe that drinking raw wine is not punishable and that punishment of hell could be inferred by a mental process.

ISKAFIS. Followers of Muhammad ibn-Abdallah al-Iskafi. They believe that Allah has power to oppress children and madmen but not those who have their full senses.

THAMAMIS. Followers of Thamamah ibn-Ashras al-Numairi. They believe that he whom Allah does not compel to know Him, is not compelled to know and is classed with animals who are not responsible.

JAHIZIS. Followers of Amr ibn-Bahr al-Jahiz. They believe that Allah is able to create a thing but unable to annihilate it.

SHAHHAMIS/SIFATIS. Followers of Abu-Yaqub al-Shahham. They believe that everything determined is determined by two determiners, one the Creator and the other acquirer.

KHAIYATIS/MAKHLUQIS. Followers of Abu-al-Husain al-Khaiyat. They believe that everything non-existent is a body before it appears, like man before it is born is a body in non-existence. Also that every attribute becomes existent when it makes its appearance.

KABIS. Followers of Abu-Qasim Abdullah ibn-Ahmad ibn-Mahmud al-Banahi known as al-Ka'bi. They believe that Allah does not see Himself nor anyone else except in the sense that He knows Himself and others.

JUBBAIS. Followers of Abu-Ali al-Jubbai. They believe that Allah obeys His servants when He fulfils their wish.

BAHSHAMIS. Followers of Abu-Hashim. They believe that one who desires to do a bad deed, though may not do it, commits infidelity and deserves punishment.

IBRIS. They believe that Holy Prophet (pbuh) was a wise man but not a prophet.

MUHKAMIS. They believe that God has no control over His creations.

QABARIS. They do not believe in the punishment of grave.

HUJJATIS. They do not believe in the punishment for deeds on the grounds that because everything is determined so whatever one does s/he is not responsible for it.

FIKRIS. They believe that doing Dhikr and Fikr (Remembering and thinking about Allah) is better than worship.

ALIVIS/AJARIS. They believe that Hadhrat Ali share prophethood with Muhammad (pbuh).

TANASIKHIS. They believe in the re-incarnation of soul.

RAIIS. They believe that Hadhrat Ali ibn-abi-Talib will return to this world.

AHADIS. They believe in the Fardh (obligations) in faith but deny the sunnah.

RADEEDIS. They believe that this world will live forever.

SATBIRIS. They do not believe in the acceptance of repentance.

LAFZIS. They believe that Quran is not the word of God but only its meaning and essence is the word of God. Words of Quran are just the words of narrator.

ASHARIS. They believe that Qiyas (taking a guess) is wrong and amounts to disbelief.

BADA'IS. They believe that obedience to Ameer is obligatory no matter what he commands.

APPENDIX B

Daffodils	Sonnet from the Portuguese XLII
William Wordsworth	**Elizabeth Browning**
I WANDER'D lonely as a cloud That floats on high o'er vales and hills, When all at once I saw a crowd, A host, of golden daffodils; Beside the lake, beneath the trees, Fluttering and dancing in the breeze. Continuous as the stars that shine And twinkle on the Milky Way, They stretch'd in never-ending line Along the margin of a bay: Ten thousand saw I at a glance, Tossing their heads in sprightly dance. The waves beside them danced; but they Out-did the sparkling waves in glee: A poet could not but be gay, In such a jocund company: I gazed—and gazed—but little thought What wealth the show to me had brought: For oft, when on my couch I lie In vacant or in pensive mood, They flash upon that inward eye Which is the bliss of solitude; And then my heart with pleasure fills, And dances with the daffodils.	My future will not copy fair my past— I wrote that once; and thinking at my side My ministering life-angel justified The word by his appealing look upcast To the white throne of God, I turned at last, And there, instead, saw thee, not unallied To angels in thy soul ! Then I, long tried By natural ills, received the comfort fast, While budding, at thy sight, my pilgrim's staff Gave out green leaves with morning dews impearled. I seek no copy now of life's first half: Leave here the pages with long musing curled, And write me new my future's epigraph, New angel mine, unhoped for in the world.

2

Islam and the Hexagon of Religious Pluralism

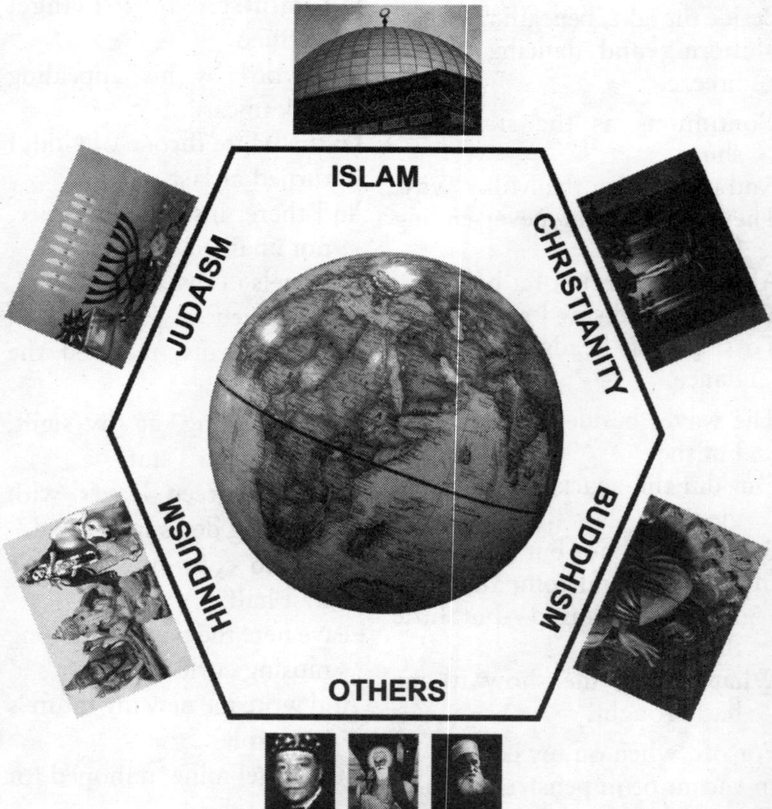

THE HEXAGON

When we look at a snap shot of the global population, we find that the majority is intertwined in a hexagon of religious beliefs. The principal links of this hexagon are Islam, Christianity, Judaism, Hinduism, Buddhism, and others such as Bahai, Sabaeans, Zoroastrians, Sikhs, Moonies, etc. Each arm of the hexagon is vital, a breakage of which interferes with the principles of peaceful co-existence. While there are similarities, subtle differences, and major philosophical clichés among these arms, only through a clear understanding of the Hexagon Concept, both Muslims and Non-Muslims can fulfil their obligations in making the earth a pleasant place to live in peace and harmony.

In order to fully understand the Hexagon Concept, both Muslims and Non-Muslims must first grasp the concept of religious pluralism, the importance of which has been mentioned in several verses of Quran. The most comprehensive discussion on religious pluralism has been presented by Heribert Busse.* The goal here is to expand on Busse's work because only then it will be apparent to all religious segments of our society that existence of various religious beliefs is also the will of God, and unity among the followers of these beliefs is extremely important, as it was for the Prophet (pbuh). Busse writes:

> Muhammad (pbuh) was determined to create unity—he saw a need for more pragmatic attitude towards Jews and Christians...he saw Salvation in tolerance without making the slightest of concession regarding dogma.

The dogma, of course, deals with the Islamic conduct of a Muslim from sunrise to sunset and has no impact on the pluralistic view of the religious hexagon.

We shall now examine the Quranic injunctions to understand the unity and peace process. It would be more comprehensive to put the Hexagon Concept in chronological order in light of the Quranic verses shown in Appendix C and D.

---

* *Islam, Judaism and Christianity, Theological and Historical Affliction* by Heribert Busse, published by Markus Wiener Publishers, New Jersey, USA.

ISLAM AND

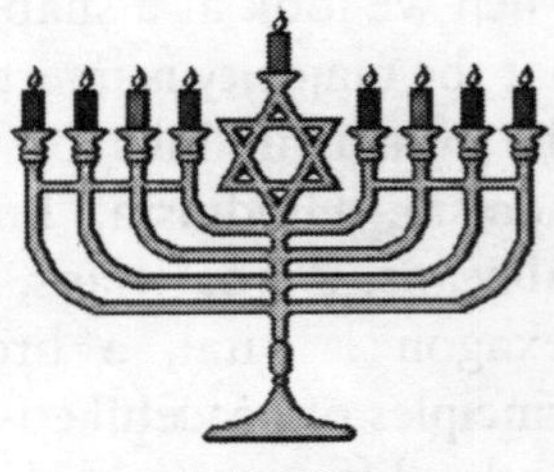

JUDAISM

Both Muslims and Jews will be rewarded by Allah for their good deeds (2:62, 5:69); they will be in the company of blessed people (4:69-70); both Muslims and Jews believe in Moses and there is no discrimination by God (2:136); God revealed both Quran and Torah (3:3, 6:155, 6:92); Quran emphasizes on the commonality of the two religions (3:3); there are righteous Jews and Muslims who recite His revelations and prostrate before Him (3:113); both are righteous people (3:114); His revelations were sent to all prophets and He spoke to Moses directly (4:163-164); Allah chose Moses to deliver His message [just as He sent Muhammad (pbuh)] (7:144); Muslims are admonished to not argue with Jews and say to them "We believe in the same God as you do" (29:46); Moses and Aaron received Allah's blessings (same as Muhammad [pbuh] did) as they were His believing devotees (as Muhammad [pbuh] was) [37:114-122]; Moses and Aaron were granted the criterion of wrong and right (just as Muhammad [pbuh] was) [21:48-49]; Jews will be given their reward twice for repelling evil (28:54); both Muslims and Jews refrain from vain talk and avoid the way of ignorance (28:55); Moses was sent by Allah (so was Muhammad [pbuh]) with His clear sign and a clear authority (40:23); Both Quran and Torah were disputed by unbelievers (41:45); Jews were chosen above the nations of the world (44:32); Torah, revealed to Moses, was a guide and blessing and Quran confirms it (46:12); both Muslims and Jews have marks on their forehead as both prostrate before One God (48:29).

Remarks

The common attributes between Muslims and Jews hardly justify any animosity or hostility. My association with my Jewish colleague Mark Buckbinder during my employment within the US defense industry was a living example of Muslim-Jew friendship. We together constituted the two important arms of the hexagon.

ISLAM AND

CHRISTIANITY

Muslims and Christians, who believe in God (Allah) and the Day of Resurrection, will be rewarded for their good deeds (2:62, 5:69); nearest to Muslims are Christians because among them are priests and monks who are God-fearing (5:82); both Muslims and Christians believe in the same God (Allah) and there is no discrimination by God (Allah) (2:133-136); both Quran and Gospel (Injeel) were revealed by Him (Allah) (3:37); Quran emphasizes on the commonality of the two religions (3:64); there are believing Muslims and Christians who recite the revelations of Allah and prostrate before Him (God) (3:113); both Muslims and Christians are righteous people and will be rewarded for their good deeds (3:114-115); God sent his revelations to both Muhammad (pbuh) and Jesus (pbuh) (4:163-164); God provides sustenance to both Muslims and Christians (6:151); any Muslim who wishes to harm Christians is considered a wrong doer (6:52); among both Muslims and Christians there are devotees who guide others with truth and establish justice (7:181); Muslims and Christians alike will bear the burden (receive Allah's punishment) for misleading the ignorant (16:25); both Muslims and Christians receive Allah's bounty (17:20); when disagreements arise, Muslims are prohibited from arguing with Christians and are admonished to respond by saying your God is the same One God to whom we submit as Muslims (29:46); it is Allah who will unite Muslims and Christians (34:26); Muslims and Christians belong to the universal brotherhood (two important arms of the hexagon) (21:92-93); Muslims and Christians alike will receive their reward as they have repelled evil and strengthened their soul (28:54); Muslims are admonished to back away from useless arguments with Christians and wish them peace (28:55); the similarity between Quran and the Gospel is denoted by the prostration marks on the forehead of both Muslims and Christians (48:29).

Jesus has been mentioned in Quran in numerous verses, and Muslims revere him as a prophet of Allah. Some of these verses are shown in Appendix C. A judicious and unbiased analysis of the Quranic verses, shown in Appendix C, offers an insight into the Islamic perception of Jesus whose nobility, righteousness, conviction to worship One God (Islam), humility, acceptance to be mortal and no more than a Messenger of God, ability to perform miracles, and return on the Day of Resurrection are unquestionable.

Most importantly, the proclamation of the coming of a Messiah (Ahmad or Muhammad) (verse 61:6) is also supported by Bible as stated in chapter 1 (prophethood of Muhammad [pbuh]).

In the interest of global peace, it is crucial to emphasize that: (A) Any anti-Islamic rhetoric, as often entertained by televangelists and talk show host, must be diffused, and (B) Any anti-Christian slogans that reverberate in mosques and Islamic convention must be toned down. After all, Muslims and Christians are integral parts of the global brotherhood and constitute two important arms of the hexagon.

ISLAM

AND

HINDUISM

While Islam and Hinduism are two distinctly different religions, and do not share any historical similarities, existence of other nations (Hindus included) is predicated in Quran (verses 5:48, 6:151, 11:119, 16:25, 16:93, 17:20, 21:92-93, 76:2-3). In spite of the monotheistic doctrine of Islam and the polytheistic mythology of Hinduism, there are certain common beliefs that both Muslims and Hindus share to strengthen their spiritualism.

For instance:

- Both Muslims and Hindus believe in life after death. Muslims will face God (Allah) on the Day of Resurrection and be assigned to paradise or hell based on their deeds. Though there is no concept of a Day of Resurrection in Hinduism, they do believe in life after death and both paradise (swarg) and hell (narak) are integral parts of the Hindu belief. As in Islam, a Hindu will enter Swarg or Narak depending on his or her Karma (deeds). The concepts of puniya (good deeds) and paap (bad deeds) are also Islamic concepts.
- As Quran emphasizes unity among the Muslim ummah, and peaceful coexistence with Non-Muslims, Mahabharat fosters unity among the Indian people and presents an embodiment of ideals.
- Both Islam and Hinduism foster non-violence (Ahimsa). A classical example is Gandhi's Ahimsa movement to gain independence from the British. The same concept adopted by Martin Luther King Jr. earned him a Nobel Peace Prize.
- As the four Muslim Imams—Malik, Hanbal, Shafii, and Abu Hanifa established the Islamic Jurisprudence, Manu composed the Shastras (Law book) setting forth the duties of Hindus.
- As Muslims are reminded again and again in the Quran and the Sharia to fight against Shaitan (devil), Hindus are reminded similarly in the Ramayan to fight against the rakshasas, daityas, yakshas, and asuras, the demons

and devils that are constantly at war with men and gods.*

- As Quran addresses protection of the dhimmies (non-Muslims), Ramayan emphasizes protection of the hermits.
- As the Prophet (pbuh) introduced the concepts of Rahma (kindness), discipline and patience, Valmiki contemplated the severity of social discipline and believed that those in power must practice the greatest self-restraint as rank imposes obligations and discipline without which power simply dissipates.*

In summary, both Muslims and Hindus can share similar virtues while practicing their own religions. Any Muslim or any Hindu who promotes the doctrine of hate and violence is out to fracture two important arms of the hexagon and must be reminded of his or her duties.

A Passing Remark

I still remember my school days in India when I used to stay up all night to help my Hindu classmates prepare for Saraswati pooja (Saraswati is the goddess of knowledge, pooja means prayer).

ISLAM AND

BUDDHISM

Both Islam and Buddhism share some common moral values in spite of being two diverse religious philosophies. Quranic

---

* *Hinduism and Buddhism* by Coomaraswamy and Ananda Kentish, published by Greenwood Publishing Group, Westport, Connecticut, USA.

verses that solidify the existence of other nations, including Buddhists, have been shown earlier. A synopsis of comparative spiritualism in both religions is presented below:

- As in Islam, Buddhism is based on the belief that present actions are linked to future consequences in this life as well as in the life hereafter.
- Both Islam and Buddhism foster the concepts of reward and punishment based on deeds. In Buddhism (as in Hinduism), Karma is classified as puniya (good deeds) and paap (bad deeds). It is the Karma that enables one to reach the Nirvana*—an eternal, pure, tranquil and deathless state. The ascension to Nirvana through a complex process of meditation and puniya (good deeds) is similar to the Islamic concept of life in paradise which will be eternal and deathless.
- The canonical doctrines of five pillars and six articles of faith in Islam, discussed earlier, are similar to the Buddhist concepts* of anupurvekatha—a process of progression that takes one to dana (selfless giving), shila (morality), swarga (heaven), and dharma-deshana (instruction on doctrine).
- The concept of "Noble Eightfold Path" in Buddhism* that strengthen spiritualism namely:

  1. Right view, 2. Right thought, 3. Right speech, 4. Right action, 5. Right livelihood, 6. Right effort, 7. Right mindfulness, 8. Right concentration. They are also Islamic concepts and integral parts of an Islamic way of life.
- The five moral codes* in Buddhism namely:

  1. No intentional destruction of life (anti-abortion), 2. No stealing, 3. No sexual misconduct (adultery), 4. No lying, and 5. No intoxication. They are also Islamic moral codes.

---

* *Buddhism* by Kevin Trainer, published by Oxford University Press, New York.

- The religion of Buddha has been summarized in the following verse:

  "To cease from all sins. To get virtues. To clean one's own heart."*

Cessation of sins, attainment of virtues, and cleansing of heart, have been mentioned in several places in Quran, and in this regard, both Islam and Buddhism share common beliefs. In summary, when one analyses the two religions, he/she finds many common attributes that are vital for peaceful coexistence, and it becomes apparent that the fifth arm of the hexagon (Buddhism) is as important as the remaining arms.

ISLAM AND OTHERS

NATION OF ISLAM

ZOROASTRIANISM

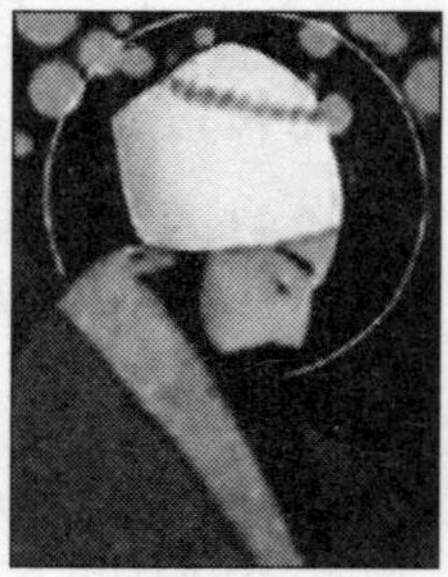

SIKHISM

THE BAHAI FAITH

Because of the large number of smaller religious and mythological sects that prevail globally, it is almost impossible

* *Hinduism and Buddhism* by Coomaraswamy and Ananda Kentish.

to enter into a comparative discussion of doctrinal and philosophical similarities with Islam. We observe Parsis (Zoroastrians) and Sikhs in India, Bahais in the United States and elsewhere, the Nation of Islam in the United States, and Moonies in the US and elsewhere, and so on. The point to emphasize herein is to recognize the fact that they constitute a significant percentage of world population. Also, if one painstakingly takes the time to research each religion and mythology, it would be found that they all live by some moral values that may or may not be in sink with Islam. But according to Quran, they will be accountable for their good or bad deeds and must be respected for what they are—the sixth arm of the hexagon.

APPENDIX C

Quran says:

2:62 Verily! Believers, Muslims, Jews, Christians, and
5:69 Sabians*—whoever believes in Allah and the Day of Resurrection and performs good deeds—will be rewarded by their Rabb; they will have nothing to fear or to regret.

They were neither Jews nor Christians.

2:133 Were you present when death approached Jacob (Yaqoob)? He asked his sons: "Who will you worship after me?" They replied: "We will worship the same One God who is your Rabb (Lord) and the Rabb (Lord) of your forefathers' Abraham (Ibrahim), Ismael (Ismail), and Isaac (Ishaq) and to Him we all submit as Muslims."

2:136 Say: We believe in Allah and that which is revealed to us; and what was revealed to Abraham (Ibrahim), Ismael (Ismail), Isaac (Ishaq), Jacob (Yaqoob) and their descendants, and that which was given to Moses (Musa), Jesus (Isa) and other prophets from their Rabb (Lord). We do not discriminate any of them.

---

* Sabians were Iraqis who believed in one God and read Az-Zabur.

3:3 He has revealed to you this Book (Quran) with the truth, confirming the scriptures which preceded it, as He revealed the Torah (Taurat) and the Gospel (Injeel).

3:64 Say: "O People of the Book! Let us get together on what is common between us and you."

3:113 There are some among the People of the Book who are upright, who recite the revelations of Allah all night long and then prostrate before Him.

3:114 These are righteous people.

3:115 Whatever good they do, its reward will not be denied to them.

4:69-70 Whosoever obeys Allah and the Rasool will be in the company of those who Allah has blessed—the prophets, the truthful, the martyrs, and the righteous what excellent companion they will be.

4:163-164 O Muhammad (pbuh), we have sent revelations to you just as we sent to Noah (Nuh) and the prophets who came after him; we also sent revelations to Abraham (Ibrahim), Ismael (Ismail), Isaac (Ishaq), Jacob (Yaqoob), his descendants Jesus (Isa), Job (Ayuh), Jonah (Yunus), Aaron (Haroon) and Solomon (Sulaiman) and to David (Dawood); we gave Psalms—to Musa (Moses) Allah spoke directly.

5:48 If Allah wanted He could have made all of you a single nation. But He willed otherwise in order to test you in what He had given you; therefore try to excel one another in good deeds. Ultimately you all shall return to Allah; then He will show you the truth of those matters in which you dispute.

5:82 And nearest to the believers (Muslims) in affection are those who say: "We are Christians." That is because among them are men that are priests and monks, who do not behave arrogantly.

6:52 You are in no way accountable for their deeds nor they are in any way accountable for yours. So if you drive them away, you shall be counted among the wrong doers.

6:92 This is the blessed Book (Quran), like the one given to Musa (Moses) confirming what came before it.

6:108 O believers (Muslims), do not insult those, whom these mushrikin call upon besides Allah—thus we have made the deeds of every group of people seems fair to them.

6:151 We provide sustenance for you and for them, not to commit shameful deeds whether openly or secretly, not to kill any soul forbidden by Allah except for the requirement of justice.

6:155 We have revealed this Book (Quran), similar to the Book given to Musa (Moses) as a blessing; therefore, follow it and adopt a God-fearing attitude so that you may receive mercy.

7:144 Allah said: "O Musa (Moses)! I have chosen you from among mankind to deliver my message and to have conversations with me.

7:181 Among those whom we have created there are some people who guide others with the truth and establish justice therewith.

11:118 If your Rabb (Lord) had so willed, He would have certainly made mankind one single nation but that is not what He wants so they will continue to differ.

11:119 And that freedom of choice and action is the whole purpose of their creation.

16:25 Let them (non-Muslims) bear their own burden in full and that of those whom they have misled in their ignorance.

16:93 If Allah wanted, He could have made you all one nation; but He let go astray whom He wants and guides whom He pleases: but most certainly you will be questioned about all your actions.

17:20 We bestowed on all-these as well as well those (implies both Muslims and non-Muslims), out of the bounties of your Rabb (Lord); the bounties of your Rabb are not confined.

17:56 Say: "Pray if you will to those whom you assert besides Him (Allah): they have neither the power to relieve you from any distress nor to change it.

21:48-49 Certainly we granted Musa (Moses) and Haroon (Aaron) the Criterion of right and wrong, a light and a reminder for those righteous people who fear their Rabb though they have not seen Him, and dread the Day of Judgment.

21:71 We delivered him (Ibrahim Abraham) and his nephew Lut (Lot) and directed them to the land which we have blessed for all the people of the world.

21:92-93 Verily this brotherhood of yours (mankind) is a single brotherhood and I am your only Rabb, therefore worship me alone. But the people have divided their religion into sects between them—to us they shall all return.

28:54 They (righteous Jews and Christians) are the ones who will be given their reward twice because they have endured with fortitude, repelling evil with good.

28:55 When they hear vain talk, they withdraw from it saying "Our deeds are for us and yours for you, peace be on to you, we do not desire the way of the ignorant.

29:46 Do not argue with the People of the Book (Jews and Christians) and say: We believe in that which is sent down to us and that which is sent down to you; our God and your God is the same One God to whom we submit as Muslims.

34:26 Say: "Our Rabb (Lord) will bring us all together, then He will rightly judge between us. He is the Judge who knows everything.

37:114-122 We bestowed our favor on Musa (Moses) and Haroon (Aaron). We delivered them with all their people from the mightly distress. We helped them so they became victorious. We gave them the Glorious Book (Torah) and guided them both to the right way. We left their good name among the later generations. Salutation to Musa and Haroon. Thus do we reward the righteous. Surely they were two of our believing devotees.

40:23 Indeed we sent Musa with our clear sign and a clear authority.

41:45 Before this Quran, we had given the Book to Musa (Moses) and it was similarly disputed.

44:32 We chose them (children of Israel—Jews), in spite of knowing their weaknesses above the nations of the world.

46:12 Yet before it (Quran) the Book of Musa was revealed which was a guide and blessing, and the Book (Quran) confirms it.

48:29 They (believers) have marks of Sajud (prostration) on the foreheads, the traces of their prostration. This is their similitude in the Taurat (Torah); and their similitude in the Injeel (Gospel).

76:2-3 Indeed, we have created man from the sperm drop containing both sexes—now it is his choice to be grateful or to be a disbeliever.

APPENDIX D

Quran says:

3:45 When the angels said "O Maryam (Mary)! Allah gives you the good news with a word from Him that you will be given a son: his name will be Messiah, Isa (Jesus) the son of Maryam. He (Jesus) will be noble in this world and the Hereafter, and he will be from those who are very close to Allah.

3:46 He will speak to the people in the cradle and in his manhood, and he will be one of the righteous.

3:47 She (Mary) said: "O my Lord! How shall I have a son when no man has touched me." He (Allah) said: "Even so Allah creates however He wants; whenever he decides to do anything, He only says to it "Be" and it is (meaning it gets done).

3:48 And He (Allah) will teach him (Jesus) the Book, the Wisdom, the Taurat (Torah and the Injeel) (the Gospel).

3:49 And make him (Jesus) a Messenger to the children of Israel with his message: "I have come to you with a sign from your Lord (Allah), that I design for you out of clay a bird and breathe into it, and by Allah's leave, it will become a living bird; and I heal the blind, and the leper, and I will bring the dead to life by Allah's Leave; and I will tell you what you have eaten and what you have stored in your houses. Surely, these are the signs to convince you if you are believers.

3:50 I am appointed to confirm that which is before me from the Taurat (Torah) and to make lawful to you some of the things forbidden to you, and I have come to you with a proof from your Lord. So fear Allah and obey me.

3:51 Truly! Allah is my Lord and your Lord. So worship Him (Allah). This is the right way.

3:54 The unbelievers among the children of Israel plotted to kill him (Jesus) and Allah devised a plan to raise him (Jesus) up.

3:55 Allah said "O Isa (Jesus) I am going to recall you (from your mission) and raise you up to Myself. I will clean you of those who rejected you and exalt your followers above the unbelievers until the Day of Resurrection; then to Me shall be your return and I shall judge those matters in which you have been disputing.

3:59 In fact, the example of the birth of Isa (Jesus) in the Sight of Allah is like the example of Adam who had no father and mother, whom He created out of dust and said to him "Be" and he was.

3:61 In fact anyone who disputes this matter (the birth of Jesus)—say "Come! Let us gather our sons and your sons, our women and your women, ourselves and yourselves, then let us earnestly pray and invoke the curse of Allah on liars.

4:156 They (unbelievers) went in their unbelief to such an extent that they uttered terrible slander against Maryam (Mary).

4:157 They (unbelievers) even say: "We have killed the Messiah, Isa (Jesus), son of Maryam (Mary), the Prophet of Allah." Whereas in fact, neither did they kill him nor did they crucify him but they thought they did because the matter was made dubious for them. They have no knowledge, they follow nothing but conjecture, certainly they did not kill him (Jesus).

4:158 Nay! The fact is that Allah took him (Jesus) up to Himself.

4:159 There is none of the People of the Book but will believe in this fact before his death, and on the Day of Resurrection Jesus will bear witness against them.

4:172 The Messiah (Jesus) never disdained to be a worshipper of Allah.

5:72 Surely they have disbelieved who say: "Allah is Christ, the son of Maryam (Mary)." But the Messiah (Jesus) said: "O children of Israel! Worship Allah, my Lord and your Lord."

5:75 The Messiah (Jesus), the son of Maryam (Mary) was no more than a Messenger; many messengers had passed away before him. His mother Maryam was a truthful woman; they both ate earthly food like other human beings.

5:78 Those among the children of Israel who disbelieved were cursed by the tongue of Dawood (David) and Isa (Jesus), the son of Maryam, because they disobeyed and counted excesses.

19:30 He (Jesus) said: "Verily I am a slave of Allah, He has given me the Scripture and made me a Prophet.

19:36 Jesus said: "And verily Allah is my Lord and your Lord. So worship Him (Alone). This is the straight path.

43:59 He (Jesus) was no more than a mortal whom we favored and made an example to the children of Israel.

43:61 And he (Jesus), the son of Maryam shall be a known sign for the Hour of Doom. Therefore, have no doubt about its coming, follow me; this is the right way.

43:63-64 And when Jesus came with clear proof, he said, "I have come to you with wisdom, and to clarify some of those things about which you have disputes, so fear Allah and obey me. Surely it is Allah who is my Lord and your Lord, so worship Him.

61:6 And remember when Isa (Jesus) the son of Maryam said: "O children of Israel! I am the messenger of Allah unto you, confirming to Torah which came before me, and to give you good news of a Messenger to come after me, whose name shall be Ahmad (another name of Muhammad)."

Islamic Deterrence to Violence

3

The readers would recall that one of the meanings of Islam is "peace".

This chapter is dedicated to an in-depth research of the Quran and the Ahadith with the sole intent of revealing the strength, weakness, and ambiguity in the arena of peace and deterrence to violence. Global terrorism in the name of Islam has given adversaries of Islam an opportunity to ridicule Islam, and label peace as hypocrisy. Although many good books have been written on this subject, Muslim authors have refrained from scrutinizing the Quran and the Ahadith. This is because they are afraid of being labeled as Mushriks (non-believers) and do not wish to face the fate of Salman Rushdie. It is, certainly, neither my desire to rewrite "Satanic Verses"* nor I possess the literary genius of Salman Rushdie to entertain such thoughts. An objective analysis of the Quran and the Ahadith, however, will be presented in the following pages to convince Islam bashers and militant Muslims that violence is not an Islamic practice.

The literal meaning of the word violence is "an act produced by unlawful, unjust, or improper force". Due to the highly conjectural and debatable interpretations of the words "unjust" and "improper", it becomes essential to look at those Islamic doctrines which render violence unlawful. For a clear understanding, violence will be classified in five categories:

1. Domestic Violence
2. Communal Violence

---

* *Satanic Verses* by Salman Rushdie (**Satanic Verses* by Salman Rushdie, is a Penguin Group Publication).

3. Religious Violence
4. Political Violence
5. Territorial Violence

DOMESTIC VIOLENCE

Both Muslim and non-Muslim families today must endure enormous internal and external pressures to excel academically, financially, socially, and spiritually. This pressure often culminates in acts of violence in one form or the other. The clash of culture in the west combined with a zeal for socio-economic fulfilment adds to the already tense family atmosphere. Parents demand academic excellence and adherence to Islamic practices; spouses squabble about their inability to keep up with the living standards of next door neighbors; and children crave to imitate and live the life of their non-Muslim school and college mates. The ultimate outcome of this tense family atmosphere is the birth of various forms of violence, both physical and emotional.

A comprehensive list of such acts, though not complete, is shown below:

- Child Abuse
- Parent Abuse
- Elopement
- Spousal Battery
- Separation and Divorce
- Extramarital Affairs
- Withdrawal of Support

CHILD ABUSE

Abuse, according to David Gil*, a well-known researcher, is any act of commission or omission by a parent, an individual, an institution, or society as a whole that deprives a child of equal rights and liberty, and/or interferes with or constrains the child's ability to achieve his or her optimal developmental potential.

---

* *The Encyclopedia of Child Abuse* by Robin and Judith Clark, published by Facts on Files of New York.

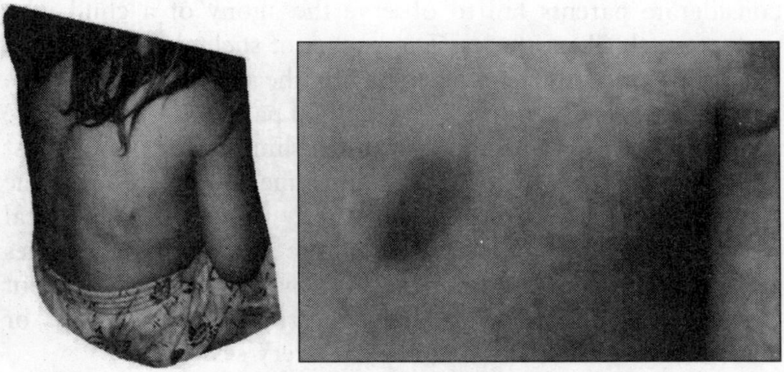

A CHILD BEATEN BY A MOTHER WITH A BELT

A superficial definition of child abuse is excessive physical punishment often resulting in injuries and occasionally death of a child. But there are numerous subtle abuses that exist among both poor and rich Muslim and non-Muslim families. These are abuses that go unnoticed and even the most loving and

A FATHER TESTS HIS MANHOOD ON A CHILD

considerate parents fail to observe the agony of a child who endures such silent abuses. The impact of such abuses could be temporary or permanent depending on the severity of the abuse. Disciplining a child for misbehaving is of paramount importance to every family, Muslim or non-Muslim. But parents must understand the difference between discipline and abuse. Discipline is a process of inculcating in them family values through logical reasoning and negotiations, whereas the same process becomes an abuse when thrust upon a child by an autocratic parent whose *modus operandi* is "spare the rod, spoil the child" or who tests his or her lung capacity in every session.

A FATHER TESTS HIS LUNG CAPACITY

A child is as vulnerable and fragile as a seedling that has just begun to sprout from a seed. For this seedling to grow into a healthy plant, one must provide proper care and nutrition; when the seedling has transformed into a small plant, it must be supported with stakes to withstand the weather and wind; to prevent the plant from wilting and dying, it must be watered when it is hot and covered when it is freezing cold; only then the plant continues to grow with healthy roots, stems, and branches. The process of raising a child is identical to growing a plant from its seed. Parents' mental faculties must be attuned to the welfare and proper upbringing of the child. As it is often said "garbage-in-garbage out", parents will reap what they sow.

The Quranic provision relating to the killing of a child has been discussed earlier (verses 6:140, 17:31, 60:12 and 81:8, 9). When one conducts an in-depth analysis of these verses, it becomes apparent that killing a child has two connotations: (a) physical death, and (b) emotional death. Granted that physical killing (infanticide) and corporal punishment resulting in a child's death are limited in scope, any Muslim who practices this horrible act does not deserve to remain alive. The emotional demise of a child takes place routinely when abusive parents magnify petty family issues and adopt a destructive course of disciplinary process. We will look at some of these petty disciplinary issues to show readers the silliness of some parents. A child gets rebuked because:

- The book bag is not in its place.
- The school assignments are taking too long or have not been done.
- The child has not prepared his/her clothes for the next day.
- Bedroom has not been arranged properly.
- House chores have not been done.
- The grade has slipped.
- Athletic performance has been substandard.
- The pet (if any) has not been given food or water.
- A visit to a friend's house has extended beyond specified time.
- It is taking a bit long to fetch a glass of water for a parent.
- The child damages a book bag or other item.
- The child suffers a minor injury.

This list can go on. What is important here, is to understand that when a child is rebuked because of no fault of his/her, the child receives an emotional blow. The impact of this emotional blow is often long lasting and shapes the personality of the child.

The child grows up to be an abusive parent. The root cause of this abusive parental behavior is a lack of understanding of the Islamic approach to discipline and a departure from adherence to the provision of Quran and Sunnah. Only when parents begin to exercise patience as prescribed in the Quran (3:200, 11:115, 39:10, and 42:43), and follow the Prophet's (pbuh) approach to life's issues, they will be able to create a family atmosphere where abusive treatment of a child is non-existent. This atmosphere, nevertheless, cannot be created without judicious allocation of time.

In our high speed Internet civilization, families are busting their backs in the acquisition of gadgets and items of luxury. This acquisition comes with a hefty price—long hours on the job or in the business, and very little time for children. Children grow up as latchkey kids whose parents have just enough time to feed them and put them to bed. They have virtually no time to conduct a rational analysis of a child's misbehavior or inability to perform a task. The net result is temper outburst and exhibition of subtle violence, practices that are totally non-Islamic.

The National Center on Child Abuse in the United States has compiled a list of the characteristics of abusive and neglectful parents*. These characteristics are shown in Appendix E.

It is, nevertheless, important to note that these characteristics are merely symptoms of abuse, and in spite of myriad of legislations and congressional acts, child abuse is a daily occurrence in the United States and elsewhere. Unfortunately, the vast number of child welfare organizations has not succeeded in eradicating child abuse. Parents, not the government and its hierarchy, have given birth to a child, and the ultimate responsibility of the child's welfare lies upon them.

The statistics** on child abuse in the United States is frightening. According to a Children's Bureau report in 2003, more than 80 per cent abusers were parents; 59 per cent of abusers were women; in 2001, around three million cases of child abuse were reported in the United States, which is about 12.2 out of 1,000 children; an estimated 1,300 children die from abusive treatment each year; in 2001, 59 per cent of abused

---

* *The Encyclopedia of Child Abuse* by Robin and Judith Clark, pp. 25-26, a Facts on File Publication, New York.

** Reported by Nancy Evans of Wild Iris Medical Education Program, New York.

children suffered neglect; 19 per cent were physically abused; 10 per cent were sexually abused; and 7 per cent were emotionally or psychologically maltreated; according to a U.S. Advisory Board on Child Abuse and Neglect report issued in 1995, 20 to 25 per cent of infant victims with shaken-baby syndrome (violent shaking of a baby by an enraged adult) die from their injury.

An Associated Press (AP) report published by Yahoo on November 23, 2004, describes the gruesome killing of a baby by the mother in Plano, Texas. The mother killed the baby by cutting off her arms. CHILD ABUSERS, MUSLIMS OR NON-MUSLIMS, SHOULD TAKE A NOTE OF IT!!

APPENDIX E

CHARACTERISTICS OF ABUSIVE AND NEGLECTFUL PARENTS/ADULTS

Abusive	Neglectful
Unconcerned; sees the child as "bad", an "evil", a "monster", or a "witch"; unacceptable or no explanation about a child's injury; uses harsh and unreasonable discipline not suited to the child's age; were abused as children; were expected to meet high demands of their parents; were unable to depend on their parents for love and nurture; cannot provide emotionally for themselves as adults; expect their children to fill their emotional void; have poor impulse control; expect rejection; have low self-esteem; are emotionally immature; are isolated, and have no support system; marry a non-emotionally supporting spouse, and the spouse passively supports the abuse.	May have a chaotic home life; may live in unsafe conditions; may abuse drugs or alcohol; may be mentally retarded; have a low IQ or a flat personality; may be impulsive and seeks immediate gratification with no regard for long-term consequences; may be motivated or employed, but unable to find or afford child care; generally have not experienced success; have emotional needs that were not met by their parents; have little motivation or skill to effect changes in their lives; tend to be passive.

THE DESTITUTES OUTSIDE A SYMPHONY HALL

PARENT ABUSE

The best portrayal of parent abuse has been presented by the Indian film industry. A recent movie titled "Baghban" (Gardener) has depicted the horrible treatment of a retired accountant and his wife by their four children and daughters-in-law. The accountant has exhausted his life's savings in fulfilling the needs and desires of his children who have grown up to be successful professionals. The retired accountant has no means to pay his rent or care for his loving wife. He asks his children for help who reluctantly agree to keep one parent for six months on a rotation basis. These children, thereby, lay the ground for parent abuse by separating two human beings who very deeply cared for each other. Both parents are subjected to a series of emotional trauma. The climax of this parent abuse is one son's refusal to have his father's broken eyeglasses repaired, and the mother assuming the role of a maid-servant in another son's home.

This gut wrenching fictional story is true to the last word. Children of our time regard their parents as a burden. While they continue to maintain an opulent lifestyle, they hardly have time to think about the needs of their aging parents, be that food, shelter, or medicine. Even in the United States, and other western countries, where retirees receive a fixed amount from their Social Security Funds, it is barely enough to make two ends meet. There is no such thing as Social Security Funds where bulk of the Muslim population is concentrated—Asia and Africa. Aging parents there, face the fate of the accountant in the Indian movie.

When we analyze the characteristics of abusive men and women (Appendix E), it becomes clear that these men and women have the propensity to be abusive to their children and to their parents alike. While they enjoy the symphonies of Mozart and Schubert in elegant symphony halls, their homeless, hungry, and sick parents endure the howling of stray street dogs. There is hardly any difference between the plight of parents and the stray street dogs—both are destitute, unsheltered, unprotected, and starved, not only for food, but care and affection as well.

Abusive Muslims, be that a man or woman, can prevent abusive treatment of their parents if they follow the guidance provided by Quran and the Ahadith.

Quran says:

> Your Rabb has decreed to you that: you shall worship none but Him, and you shall be kind to your parents; if one or both of them live to their old age in your lifetime, you shall not say to them any word of contempt nor repel them and you shall address them in kind words. (17:23)

> You shall lower to them your wings of humility and pray: "O Rabb! Bestow on them your blessings just as they cherished me when I was a little child."(17:24)
>
> We have enjoined upon men to treat his parents with kindness. With much trouble his mother bore him, and with much pain did she give him birth. His bearing and his weaning took thirty months. When he reaches the age of full strength and becomes forty years old, he says: "My Rabb! Grant me the grace that I may thank you for the favors that you have bestowed on me and on my parents—surely I turn to you in repentance and surely I am of those who are Muslims." (46:15)
>
> But he who rebukes his parents and says "Uff" (equivalent to don't bother me or get lost)...they will be told (on the Day of Resurrection): "You squandered away your good things in your earthly life and you enjoyed them for a while. Today you shall be recompensed with a punishment of humiliation because you behaved with arrogance for which you had no right during your life on earth and because of the transgression you committed." (46:17-20)

In addition to the above Quranic provisions, a number of Ahadith have been documented by Al-Bukhari, Muslim, and others, as presented by Dr. Al-Qaradawi.* An abstract of these Ahadith is as follows:

- Disobedience to parents is a great sin.
- Disobedience to parents will exclude men and women from entering the paradise.
- Disobedient men and women will be punished by Allah in their lifetime.
- Cursing a parent is a major sin.
- Serving a parent is much more important than participating in jihad and hijrah (migration) no matter how noble the cause is.

The only exception Quran makes with regards to disobedience to parents is when non-Muslim converts to Islam, and Muslim men and women who marry non-Muslims

* *The Lawful and Prohibited in Islam*, pp. 232-36, a publication of ATP, Chicago, Illinois, USA.

(see Chapter 6 for acceptable marriages) are threatened, coerced, and forced to renounce Islam or indulge in non-Islamic activities by their non-Muslim parents or in-laws.

Quran in this regard says:

> If they (non-Muslim parents or in-laws) argue with you to commit Shirk (non-Islamic practice) of which you have no knowledge, then do not obey them; however, you should still treat them kindly. (31:15)

The most important lesson that one can learn from the Quran when dealing with parents is presented in the following verse in which Luqman addressing his son says:

> O my Son! Establish Salah (prayer), enjoin good and forbid the evil. Endure with patience whatever befalls you, surely this shows your determination in conducting the affairs. (31:17)

ELOPEMENT

Elopement is a form of violence that is inflicted upon a family by young adults whose romantic endeavors are not

THE RUNAWAY BOY AND GIRL

approved by their family. The literal meaning of the word elopement is "the running away of a woman, married or unmarried, with her lover". Young Muslim and non-Muslim girls today think nothing of eloping with a boy, be he a Muslim or a non-Muslim. The hallucinating effect of infatuation deprives them of logical reasoning. The reputation of the family, the grief of the father, and the tears of the mother lose their effectiveness in the shadow of their child's ruthless romanticism.

One of the fundamental reasons for elopement of a girl within the Islamic communities is emotional deprivation caused by ascension of a male child to a superior status. This distinctly abnormal social value leaves its marks on a female child who grows up in an emotional vacuum and is ready to fall for a boy's affection, be that genuine or laced with trickery.

Ascension of a male child to a superior status is a pre-Islamic practice by the pagans of Arabia who also practiced female infanticide. Subsequently, the Prophet (pbuh) on a number of occasions, admonished equal treatment of children, be they be sons or daughters. It is sure a pity that even today, Muslims are unconsciously practicing the pagan custom of inequality among children. When this pagan practice results in elopement of their daughters, they wonder and grieve rather than look at their diversion from Islam.

Another reason for elopement is an unhappy family atmosphere where parents invest their time and energy in quarreling and bickering with each other. In so doing, they neglect the child's needs and lay the ground for elopement.

The third reason for elopement is divorce or death of the father, which often leaves a female child in the custody of the mother who, quite frequently, struggles to earn a living. Researchers may disagree with the adverse impact of maternal employment during a child's growing years, but the fact is that it takes a bite into the time that the mother must spend with her daughter. The final outcome is an emotionally neglected free bird that is ready to fly away with a perpetrator.

Parental in-fighting and divorce have been discussed in great details in Chapter 7. What is important to remember here is that

Islam fosters sanctity and permanency of marriage, detests divorce, and prescribes the recipe for raising children whose emotional attachment with and respect for parents prevent them from elopement.

Elopement may have a happy ending in Hollywood and Bollywood movies, but in real life, it is a tragedy plagued with multitude of social, economical, and medical nightmares. Zina (adultery), illegitimate pregnancy, sexually transmitted diseases, demise of education, poverty, renunciation of religious values, litigation, alcoholism, drug abuse, prostitution, communal riots, doubtful future of siblings, and suicide are some of the many adverse outcomes of elopement. Elopement, in a nutshell, is a departure from Islamic values, and contains elements that destroy the individual and the family. A Muslim does not require the services of sociologists and psychologists to curtail family crises such as elopement. The panacea lies in the Quran and the Ahadith. In the cave of Hera, the Prophet (pbuh) was asked by Gabriel to read which eventually gave the Muslims the best "How to Fix" manual in the form of Quran. "Read" and "Follow" are the only words that both Muslim parents and their children need to memorize to cure the ills of the modern civilization. Non-Muslims can also learn a lot by studying this marvel of Islam called Quran.

SPOUSAL BATTERY

Battery, by definition, is an unlawful beating of a person. In our time, this act of violence is not limited to men who beat their wives; many husbands are subjected to this shameless practice by wives as well. Physical violence against a spouse is an outcome of a deteriorating marriage. The worst example of spousal battery in the twentieth century was the slaying of Nicole Simpson allegedly by her estranged husband, O.J. Simpson, a Heisman Trophy winning American football Super Star (although not found guilty in a criminal trial, a civil court found him responsible for Nicole's murder).

The reasons for marital deterioration are the loss of love, compassion, respect and trust for each other caused by both

NICOLE SIMPSON

O.J. SIMPSON (THEN)

HEISMAN TROPHY

O.J. SIMPSON (NOW)

THE ULTIMATE SPOUSAL BATTERY
(PHOTOGRAPHS: COURTESY OF *TIME MAGAZINE*)

internal and external circumstances as well as unfounded accusations. How does a spouse become abusive and resorts to violence is a subject that requires an entire book. What is important is to isolate the root cause of disagreements between spouses through a process of elimination utilizing simple troubleshooting techniques which emphasize four question words: what, where, when and how. Once the root cause is identified, both husband and wife must strive to correct it in light of the practices of the Prophet (pbuh) who believed in Rahma (kindness). Granted that Quran, in extraordinary circumstances permits isolation and beating of a wife (4:15 and 4:34); these are practices that were not dear to the Prophet (pbuh) and have been discussed in Chapter 6.

Beating of a husband by a wife is not addressed in Islamic Scriptures. However, in light of verse 4:34 which says, "the righteous women are devoutly obedient to their husbands," it may be concluded that this demeaning practice is unlawful (haram) in Islam. A liberated Muslim woman, however, may take advantage of this silence, and convince herself that beating of a husband is acceptable. Both husband and wife, nevertheless, must be aware that regardless of the Quranic provisions and their interpretations, spousal battery is a crime in most countries and must be avoided.

SEPARATION AND DIVORCE

Separation and divorce are acts of subtle violence that one spouse inflicts on the other. Both separation and divorce have a domino effect on a person's behavior pattern, and lead to a series of maladjusted events. Depression, alcoholism, sleepless nights resulting in various ailments, obesity, suicidal tendencies, loss of motivation, loss of finance, child custody battle, loss of children, secession of parent-child relationship, adultery, homosexuality, lesbianism, drug dependency, and various other sociological and psychological ills engulf a separated and divorced person, specially in the late stages of his or her life. In spite of struggling hard to go on with life, lingering memories continue to thrust one in emotional see-saw and psychological doldrums.

Islamic perspective of Separation and Divorce has been discussed in detail in Chapter 7. In retrospect, Islam abhors separation and divorce. Both husband and wife must exhaust all avenues of reconciliation and refrain from an impulsive action when it comes to separating from a spouse who has showered his or her love, affection, and support. The road to divorce is pretty rocky, and sleeping alone after sharing a bed with a spouse is no fun.

EXTRAMARITAL AFFAIRS

Extramarital affair is a curse that has haunted men and women since pre-Islam. Both ordinary people and famous personalities have engaged in this practice only to inflict pain and sorrow upon their spouses. The legacy of Bill Clinton, the 42nd President of the United States of America, will always be tainted with his affair with Monica Lewinsky; lawyers and judges will always cite the outcome of basket ball star Koby Bryant's rape case; and history will always remember Prince Charles' and Princess Diana's extramarital affairs.

A psychoanalysis of human behavior that leads to extramarital affair is complex and beyond the scope of this book. Ironically, it is a sociological problem that exists in all societies, Islamic or non-Islamic. In the East where Muslims are concentrated, it is mostly confined to men, whereas in the West, women are as active as men in extramarital affairs. Those of us who have seen the Hollywood movie "Doctors' Wives" and the recent serial "Desperate House Wives" can, certainly, attest to this demeaning practice.

While wives sulk within the four walls of their houses, husbands enjoy the jingles of a dancer's dancing bells and 'voluptuous expose' of her physique; while the wives sleep alone on cold beds, husbands warm the beds of mistresses and prostitutes; while wives patiently wait for their husbands' return from a trip to the West, husbands spend their nights in glittering strip clubs admiring the shape of the lap dancers' bare breasts and stuffing dollar bills in her panty; and while husbands are away from home, wives seek sexual pleasures from other male members of the family or outsiders.

The scenario presented above, is only a tip of the iceberg. There are numerous forms of extramarital activities in which men and women engage themselves to hurt each other. It is a type of violence that not only tears the husband and wife apart, but also lays the ground for the destruction of the family. Extramarital affair is nothing but adultery punishable in accordance with Islamic laws stated in Chapter 6. The Quran has provided ample guidance (*see* 3:156, 3:149, 5:5, 8:25, 11:114, 12:33, 17:32, 23:5, 23:7, 24:3, 24:33, 24:39, 3:196, 3:197, 24:21). It is up to a believer to shape his or her life in accordance with the provisions of the Quran and the Ahadith.

WITHDRAWAL OF SUPPORT

Withdrawal of support is a two-edged sword that inflicts two-sided trauma on an individual or individuals.

1. Trauma caused by withdrawal of financial support.
2. Trauma caused by withdrawal of emotional support.

Financial Support

There are usually nine groups of individuals who require financial support from relatives:

(a) Divorced or battered women who have never worked.
(b) Minor children of divorced families.
(c) Children who are in college or professional institutions.
(d) Widows whose husbands have not left behind enough for them to live on.
(e) Adult children who are unemployed.
(f) Unemployed head of household.
(g) Aging parents and in-laws.
(h) Grandparents.
(i) Unemployed siblings.

No doubt, every relative in a family is not in a position to provide financial support which is vital for the short-term survival of the members in the above groups. It is a pity, however, that those who are well-to-do, also turn their backs, and pretend as though they are ready to help but their wallets and checkbooks remain closed.

Financial support to a family member in distress is neither a legal nor a moral requirement as both legality and morality can be twisted to suit an individual agenda. It is an Islamic requirement which a believer fulfils to the best of his or her ability. Without this support, children go to bed hungry, dreams are shattered, and lives are lost. All the wealth that one accumulates; all the real estate that one purchases; all the gold and diamonds that one includes in his or her portfolio; and all the expensive rugs and furnishing that one collects to beautify his or her living, will be worthless on the Day of Resurrection. That will be the Day when the Almighty will hand out their final report card in which the liabilities will be greater than the assets, rendering them ineligible for a place in the paradise. Addressing the hypocrites and misers, Quran says:

> Be good to your parents, kinfolks, orphans, and the helpless—Allah does not love those who are arrogant and boastful (4:36);

who are themselves stingy and enjoin others to be stingy, who hide the bounties Allah has bestowed upon them. For such unbelievers we have prepared a disgraceful punishment. (4:37)

Emotional Support

Cessation of emotional support is a form of violence that affects an individual much more than withdrawal of financial support. An analysis of the causes of this withdrawal leads to three main conclusions:

(a) Sibling rivalry plays an important role in creating emotional detachment. This rivalry is generally attributed to false conception of superior intellect, superior academic achievement, higher standard of living, looks and beauty, selection of spouse, achievement of children, and the magnitude of arrogance.

(b) Division of the family, caused by divorce, separation, death of a spouse, and remarriage, has often led to severe conflicts among family members. These conflicts normally arise from petty issues, and transform into major crises, causing a breakage of the bond that keeps a family together. Love is replaced by hate, and the process of emotional detachment begins. Family members adopt a "could not care less" attitude and withdraw their emotional support for each other leaving the door wide open for a perpetrator to walk in and take advantage of the family's emotional upheaval.

(c) When a Muslim man or a woman, brought up in the West or with Western influence, rejects a potential candidate for marriage approved by the parents, or ends up choosing someone who is racially, religiously, academically, and financially different, the family home becomes a battleground. The ultimate outcome is bitter feud among family members, and cessation of emotional ties. This emotional breakdown provides an outsider and his or her family an opportunity to cash in, and steer the emotionally tormented person in a totally non-Islamic direction often leading to conversion to another religion and giving birth to a new generation of non-Muslims.

The desire to alienate a family member emotionally, is an ailment which no psychologist or psychiatrist can cure. The magical potion to cure this disease lies within Quran and Ahadith. Repeatedly Quran has imposed prohibitions against jealousy, arrogance, hypocrisy, discontent, undue indulgence in material possession, isolationism, neglect, animosity, brutality, maliciousness, departure from tawhid, marriage to non-Muslims, conversion to another religion, adultery, disobedience, rationalization (anti-Islamic), intolerance, inequality, injustice, impatience, boastfulness, demonizing, and various other ills that cause a Muslim to become an Emotionless Robot. The potion to cure these ills—"READ and FOLLOW" the Quran and make the best effort to follow the examples of the Prophet (pbuh).

COMMUNAL AND RELIGIOUS VIOLENCE

Any discussion of communal and religious violence will be incomplete without looking at the global picture. The hot spots of such violence are:

Hindu-Muslim Riots in India
Hindu-Sikh Riots in India
Shia-Sunni Riots in Pakistan, India and Iraq
Muhajir-Ansar Riots in Pakistan
Muslim-Christian Riots in Pakistan
Muslim-Christian Riots in Nigeria
Catholic-Protestant Riots in Ireland
Black-White Riots in USA
Asian-White Riots in Great Britain
Chechnyan-Russian Riots in Chechnya
Palestinian-Israeli Riots in Gaza
Tribal Fighting in Afghanistan
Muslim-Christian Riots in the Philippines
Tribal Massacre in Rwanda
Kurd-Arab Conflict in Iraq
Bengali-Bihari Conflict in Bangladesh

Tamil-Sri Lankan Conflict in Sri Lanka

Arab-African Conflict in Sudan

Muslim-Buddhist Riots in Thailand

The above list can go on. When one analyses the root cause of the world events, only one reason stands out, "territorial sovereignty". Just as a lion, the king of the jungle, does not tolerate an infringement of his territory, human mind perceives a pseudo-territorial autonomy over which he desires total control.

LION: THE KING OF THE JUNGLE

When this control is threatened by invasive elements, such as religion, race, economic deprivation, clash of ideologies, and dilution of power, the zeal for self-preservation becomes obsessively stronger resulting in violence. At this point, all lessons in canonical values, mythological decencies, racial equality, and spiritual piety are forgotten. Man becomes a lion, satisfies his appetite, and quenches his thirst with the flesh and blood of another human being. Every stroke of his weapon, every sound of his bullet, and every pop of his Molotov cocktail conveys only one message:

"YOU DO NOT BELONG HERE."

We have observed reinforcement of this territorial sovereignty in the form of the Great Wall of China, concrete walls in Palestine, No Fly Zone in Iraq, LOC (Line of Control) between India and Pakistan, DMZ (Demilitarized Zone) in Korea, and the Berlin Wall in Germany.

Backed up by barbed wire and tank barriers, an East German police officer stands guard while a bricklayer repairs damage to the Berlin Wall near Bernauer Strasse May 26, 1962. The wall was damaged by several explosions overnight.

THE BERLIN WALL
(PHOTOGRAPH: COURTESY OF *TIME MAGAZINE*)

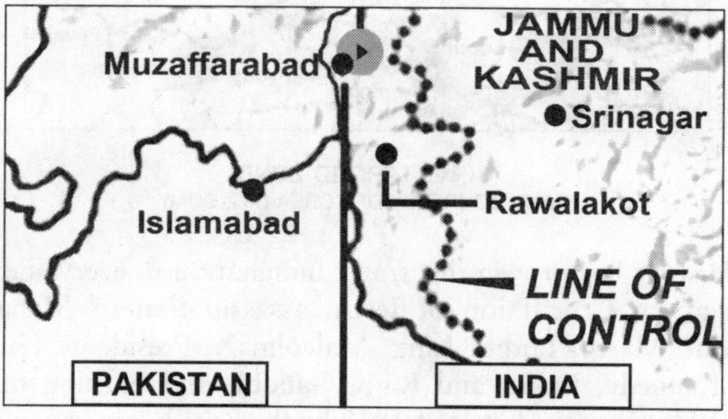

LINE OF CONTROL
(MAP: COURTESY OF *THE NEW YORK TIMES*)

THE GREAT WALL OF CHINA
(SHIN DYNASTY'S PROTECTION AGAINST THE HUANS)

DEMILITARIZED ZONE
(MAP: COURTESY OF KOREA-DMZ.COM)

History has proven this tragic indignation in every stage of civilization. Crucifixion of Jesus, assassination of Mahatma Gandhi, Martin Luther King, Malcolm X, Presidents Lincoln and Kennedy, Indira and Rajiv Gandhi, and burning of the White House in the battle of 1812 by the British, are testimonies that are engraved on the tombstone of human barbarism.

And they crucified him, and set up over his head his accusation written
THIS IS JESUS KING OF JEWS (Bible: St. Matthew)
CRUCIFIXION OF JESUS
(PHOTOGRAPH: COURTESY OF OK.KNIGHTS.ORG)

THE ASSASSINATED

As it is said "It takes two to tango" or "it takes two hands to clap," behind every act of violence, there is a victim and an executioner. The victim's action, irrespective of its nobility, clashes with the mindset of the executioner, and *vice versa*, resulting in violence and bloodshed.

THE GRAND EXECUTIONERS
(PHOTOGRAPH: COURTESY OF *TIME MAGAZINE*)

A classical example in our time is the destruction of the Babri Masjid (Mosque of Babar) by Hindu extremists. Hindu extremists believed that Babar, a Moghul emperor, had built the mosque at a spot where a temple commemorating the birth place of Lord Rama had stood at Ayodhya in India. Undoubtedly, this is a deplorable act and has led to a wave of Hindu-Muslim riots. But Muslims have done the same. Islamic jurisprudence had taken a back seat when the Talibans, whose atrocities are documented in *Zoya's Story**, destroyed centuries-old statues of Buddha in Afghanistan in the twentieth century, and Mehmud of Ghazni destroyed and looted Hindu temples in the eleventh century.

---

* *Zoya's Story* by Zoya, John Follain, Rita Cristofari, published by Harper Collins.

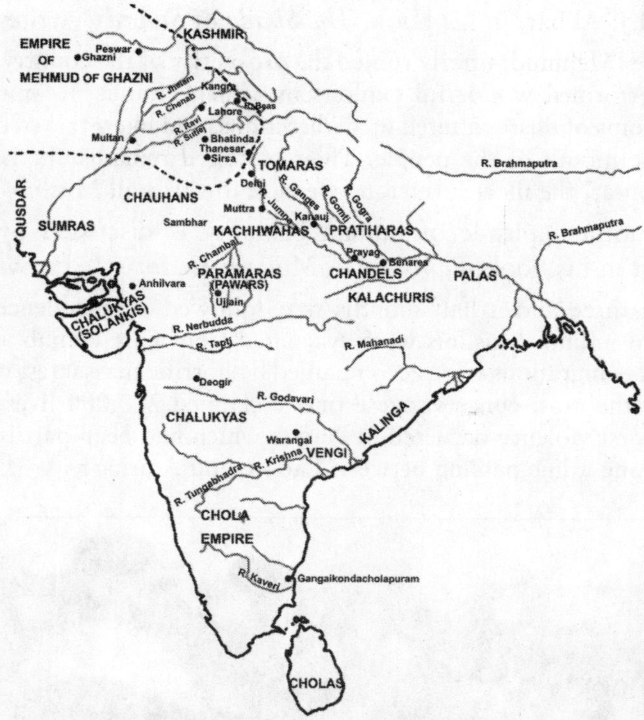

MEHMUD GHAZNI'S CONQUEST OF INDIA
(MAP: COURTESY OF ALLWONDERS.COM)

TYPICAL STATUE OF BUDDHA DESTROYED BY THE TALIBAN
(PHOTOGRAPH: COURTESY OF *TIME MAGAZINE*)

M.J. Akbar, in his book, *The Shade of Swords** writes:

> He (Mehmud) utterly ruined the prosperity of the country, and performed wonderful exploits by which Hindus became like atoms of dust scattered in all directions, and like a tale of old in the mouth of the people. Their scattered remains cherish, of course, the most inveterate aversion towards all Muslims.

Another episode of human brutality is discussed by Ian Talbot in his book, *Pakistan: A Modern History***. He writes:

> In three and a half months that followed independence***, 4.6 million Muslims were evacuated from East Punjab alone. The migrations were accompanied by horrific massacres, which at the most conservative estimate claimed 200,000 lives. The worst violence occurred in Punjab which had been partitioned along a line passing between Lahore and Amritsar.

MUSLIM MIGRATION FROM INDIA TO PAKISTAN
(PHOTOGRAPH: COURTESY OF *PAKISTAN, A MODERN HISTORY* BY IAN TALBOT)

Looking back into the history of India, the two nation concept emerged from the distrust of Muslims by the British

---

* *The Shade of Swords,* p. 103, a Routledge Publication.

** *Pakistan: A Modern History* by Ian Talbot, p. 101, a St. Martin's Press Publication.

*** August 15, 1947 for India, and August 14, 1947 for Pakistan.

Raj. The root cause of this distrust was the mutiny of 1857 when Muslim sepoys (police) attempted to restore Bahadur Shah II as emperor, which was, of course, foiled. Subsequent events led to the creation of Muslim League and Jamiat-ul-Ulma-i-Islam (Association of the Scholars of Islam). These two organizations vehemently fought for the creation of a Muslim state. India was, ultimately, divided against the reluctance of Mahatma Gandhi, and Pakistan emerged under the leadership of Qaid-e-Azam (the great leader) Jinnah. This division, not only divided territory, but also the hearts of Muslims and Hindus, and sowed the seed for frequent Hindu-Muslim riots, Gandhi's assassination, and numerous wars between India and Pakistan, the chronicle of which has been presented by Ian Talbot and other writers. One thorny issue left unresolved by the British Raj, was the future of Muslim dominated Kashmir which has been a disputed territory since 1947. A failure of the two governments (India and Pakistan) to settle this issue has given birth to Kashmiri militant groups that are engaged in armed conflict with the Indian army to gain independence. Until this issue is resolved, the magnificent landscape of Kashmir will continue to remain soaked with the blood of both Muslims and Hindus.

Ironically, human mind is quick to ignore its past misgivings and adopts a course that is a deterrent to peaceful coexistence with others. Self-serving community leaders thrive on the communal and tribal dissensions. Their aim is to exploit the rank-and-file population by feeding religious and racial fervors that often have no relevance with religion or race. Until these selfish morons grow up to be men and recognize the value of peace, loss of human life as well as human dignity will go on, and the souls of Muhammad (pbuh), Jesus (pbuh), Moses (pbuh), Buddha, and the Hindu god and goddesses will continue to ache.

Both Muslims and non-Muslims can learn a lot by studying the Quran, and the convictions of Prophet Muhammad (pbuh) and his true followers, who abhorred violence except in self-defense.

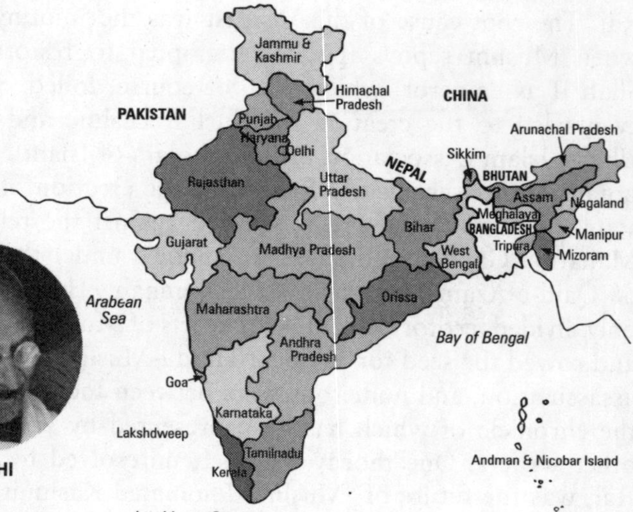

GANDHI

INDIA AFTER PARTITION

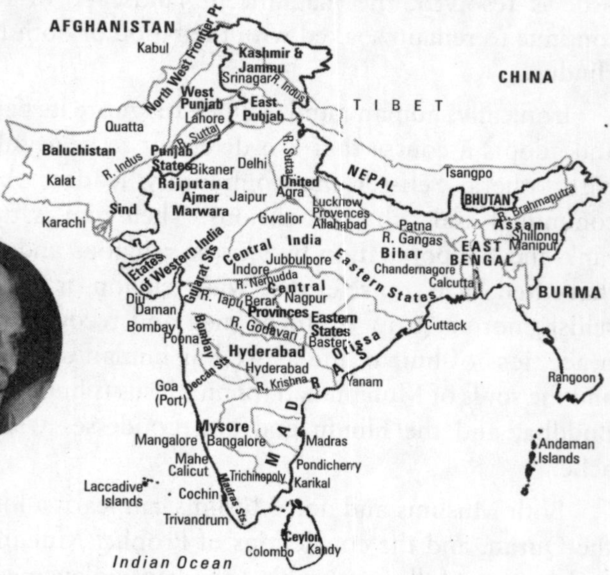

JINNAH

INDIA BEFORE PARTITION

PARTITION OF TERRITORY AND HEARTS

Quran says:

> We ordained for the children of Israel that whoever kills a person, except as a punishment for murder or mischief in the land, it will be written in his book of deeds as if he killed all the human beings on the surface of the earth, and whoever will save a life shall be regarded as if he gave life to all human beings on the surface of the earth. (5:32)

The chronology of M.J. Akbar's book leads one to read about the Islamic justice of Saladin who united the Muslims in 1187 AD and regained Jerusalem that had been lost to Christian crusaders. The noteworthy points of his conquest are as follows:

- Not a single Christian was killed and Jerusalem was taken without bloodshed.
- Freed hundreds of poor men and women without ransom money.
- Released widows and wives of prisoners.
- Allowed Syrian and Armenian Christians to live on in Jerusalem.
- Prohibited destruction of any church including the church of the Holy Sepulcher.
- He invited the Jews back into the city; Jews were given homes and built a Synagogue with his approval.
- Saladin emulated the approaches of Umar, the caliph, who had visited Jerusalem in or around 637 AD when Muslims had conquered Jerusalem from Sophoronius. Umar had declined to pray in the church of the Holy Sepulcher when he was touring the church with Sophoronius. He was afraid that his prayer may encourage Muslims to convert the church into a mosque.

It is hoped that the above discussion will convey to both Muslims and non-Muslims that:

(a) Islam does not condone useless killing.
(b) Islam does not encourage destruction of places of worship.
(c) Islamic jurisprudence is alive to serve all.

POLITICAL VIOLENCE

The political violence in Islam has its roots dating back to 632 AD when the Prophet (pbuh) had died, and Abu Bakr was chosen to be the first Khalifah (Caliph) against the wishes of Ali, the son-in-law of the Prophet (pbuh). This event laid the ground for dissension among Muslims and divided them into two major sects—Sunnis and Shias. The heinous impact of this sectarian division is present to this date, and the two sects find it difficult to coexist with one another as seen recently in Iraq, Pakistan and India.

One often hears praises of the early Muslims. Examples of their piety, and devotion to the Prophet (pbuh), are repeated time and time again in Friday prayers and Islamic conventions. Hardly anyone discusses their dissensions. One important aspect of human weakness that Muslims often forget or ignore, is the desire to retain power and rise above everybody else. They squabble on petty issues, such as naming of a school or a mosque, saying Amen silently or loudly, marrying a daughter immediately after the first menstrual period, who must be excluded from a marriage or graduation ceremony, and a myriad of other issues that hardly contribute in the global uplift of the Muslim ummah. The seed that was planted in Abu Bakr's time still produces bitter dissensions and disagreements among Muslims. The Prophet (pbuh) would definitely not encourage such division as unity of the Muslim ummah was very dear to him. The concept of unity is stressed in Quran.

Quran says:

> O believers! All together hold fast to the rope of Allah and be not divided among yourselves. (3:103)
>
> Be not like those who became divided into sects and who started to argue against each other after clear revelations had come to them.
>
> Those responsible for division and arguments will be sternly punished. (3:105)

Unfortunately in today's political climate, the above Quranic verses have lost their impetus. Klashnikovs have replaced Islamic wisdom. Factional disagreement and Al-Qaeda support in Waziristan; ideological differences in Iraq and Iran; violence in Afghanistan, Palestine, Saudi Arabia, Jordon, Indonesia, Egypt, Pakistan, Thailand, the Philippine, United Kingdom, Russia, India; and ethnic cleansing by government supported Arab militia in the Darfur region of Sudan, have precipitated crucifixion of Islamic doctrine by none but Muslims. The Talibans have forgotten their lessons in Islam, Osama-bin-Laden's Al-Qaeda has twisted Wahabi and Sufi principles, and the others are helping strengthen the "Islam and Sword" chronicle of Edward Gibbons.

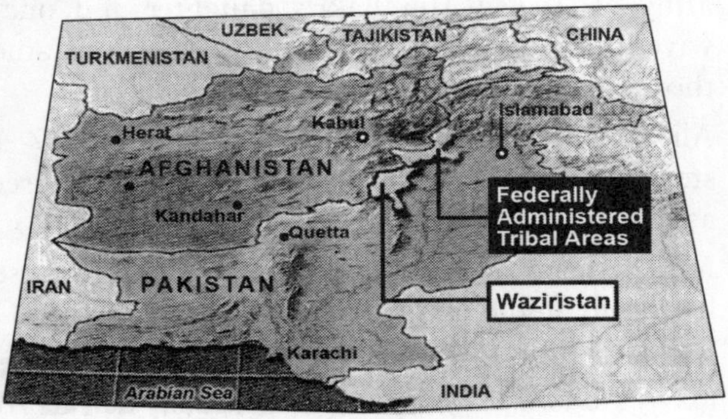

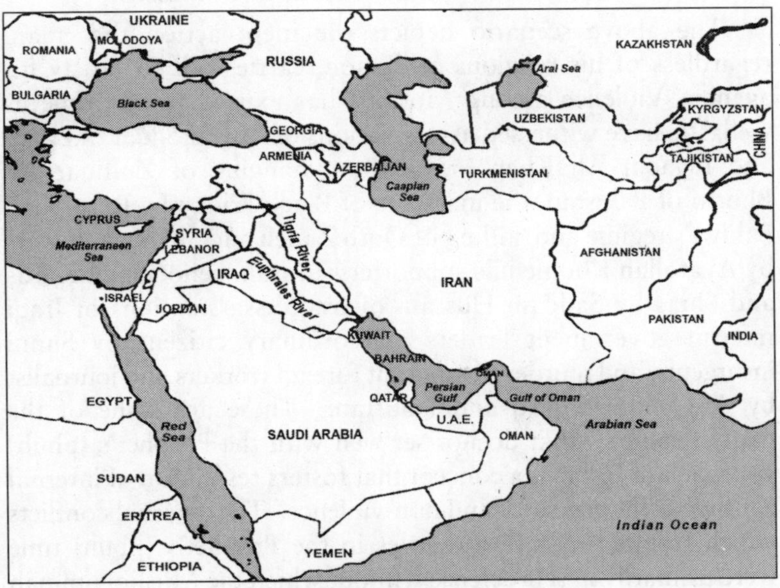

THE AL-QAEDA SYMPATHY ZONE

Muslims, in retrospect, have been engaged in political violence for many centuries. A chronology of early political violence presents the following scenario:

- Dissension among Muslims started in or around 632 AD.

- Uthman, the third Caliph is assassinated in or around 656 AD.
- Ali is finally chosen as the fourth Caliph but faces the army of Aisha (Abu Bakr's daughter and one of the wives of the Prophet (pbuh) in the Battle of Camel when thousands of Muslims die.
- Ali encounters the forces of Muawiya in 657 AD and steps down to end the civil war. He is subsequently assassinated by one of his own followers.
- Muawiya's son Yazid massacres Ali's son Hussein and his family in the Battle of Karbala in or around 680 AD.
- Abdal Malik* became Caliph in 684 but faces rebellion led by Abdallah. Abdal Malik eventually defeats Abdallah and displays his head on a spear in Damascus.

The above scenario depicts the inept action that man, regardless of his religious affiliation, carries out to satisfy his agenda. Violence among Muslims has existed in our time as well. We have witnessed assassinations of Anwar Sadat of Egypt and Liyaqat Ali Khan of Pakistan, hanging of Zulfiqar Ali Bhutto of Pakistan, the massacre of Black Friday by Reza Shah Pahlwi's regime and killing of Qutb Zadeh and Shah's followers by Ayatollah Khomeini's supporters in Iran, genocide of Kurds and Shias by Saddam Hussain of Iraq, assassinations of Iraqi interim government leaders and ordinary citizens by Sunni insurgents, and murder of innocent foreign workers and journalist by Al-Qaeda in Iraq and Pakistan. These are some of the many examples that do not set well with the Prophet's (pbuh) approach of Rahma, a concept that fosters resolution of internal conflicts with prudence and non-violence. The external conflicts which resulted in several battles in the Prophet's (pbuh) time were primarily in self-defense without which the Muslim ummah would become extinct. Political violence, under the banner of Islam with the sole intent of bolstering personal image, and satisfying selfish ambitions, is anti-Islamic, and a diversion from Islamic values.

---

* The Dome of the Rock was constructed during his caliphhood.

TERRITORIAL VIOLENCE

Territorial violence has provided the literary elites a phenomenal opportunity to express their views, and many publications under the titles "Jihad" and "Terrorism" have emerged. The number of such publications is steadily rising since the sad events of 9/11 when Osama-bin-Laden's partisans destroyed the World Trade Center in New York and damaged the Pentagon in Washington, DC. Before a discussion on territorial violence can be undertaken, it is important that we understand connotations of words that have shaped the thinking of Muslims and non-Muslims globally.

Territory:	Any separate tract of land that belongs to a state, city, or other body.
Violence:	An act produced by unlawful, unjust, or improper force.
Terrorism:	An act of intimidation.
Terrorist:	A person who rules by intimidation.
Occupation:	An act of taking possession.
Liberation:	An action to free (land, society, humanity, etc.).
Insurgency:	The state of being rebellious.
Mutiny:	A resistance to or revolt against the government.
Civil War:	A war between the people of the same state.
Jihad:	A spiritual struggle for self-purification. A military struggle in self-defense.
Jihadi (Jihadist):	One who engages in Jihad.
Fedain:	Those who willingly lay down their life for others.
Aatankwadi:	An Indian word for terrorist.

The Lion King's analogy of territorial sovereignty, when put in the proper perspective, will explain the sources of violence that have existed since the early days of Islam and prevailed in the twentieth and the twenty-first centuries. Territorial violence in our time can be grouped in two major subgroups:

Muslims vs. Muslims

Muslims vs. Non-Muslims

The most comprehensive chronological portrayal of Muslim conquests and defeats that shed light on territorial violence has been presented by M.J. Akbar in his book, *The Shade of Swords*, (pp. 239-50). A careful analysis of events leads one to observe that while there have been a few scrimmages where Muslims have fought Muslims to gain control of a territory, majority of the battles have been fought between Muslims and Christians, between Muslims and Jews, between Muslims and Hindus and lately between Muslims and a coalition of non-Muslim armies. Some of the few confrontations involving Muslims only are:

- Moorish Sultan vs. Moors and Arabs (903-910)
- Taimuer vs. Byezid (1402)
- Selim vs. Maubiks (1517)
- Babar vs. Ibrahim (1526)
- Sher Shah Suri vs. Humayun (1540)
- Ottoman Sultan Mahmud II vs. Wahabis (1812-1819)
- East Pakistani Bengalis vs. The Government of Pakistan (1971 when Bangladesh is created).
- Iraq vs. Iran (1980-1988)
- Talibans vs. Forces of Mehmoud (1996)
- Iraq vs. Kuwait (1998)

Had the Muslims understood the true meaning of Jihad *i.e.* self-purification, these confrontations would not have taken place. But history has shown that Muslims have kept their Quran and Ahadith covered in glittering silk and brocade cases and carried on atrocities against each other. These atrocities are sure to put them in red as far as their final profit and loss statement is concerned.

In order to understand the Muslim-Non-Muslim conflicts, one needs to know who the Muslims are. In essence, they are early converts and their descendants who have gone through the process of Islamization based on the Quran, the Ahadith, and the local traditions. This process of Islamization started with the pagans of Arabia and filtered down to the Christians, Jews, Mongols, Zoroastrians, and Hindus over a period of more than fourteen hundred years.

The architect of Islamic expansionism was Muawiya whose accomplishments have been very well documented by

M.J. Akbar. The seven crusades between Muslims and Christians, anti-Christian and anti-Jewish verses in Quran, documentation of Jewish betrayal and continued reminder thereof by Muslim clergy, the rise and fall of the Mongols, the battles between Moghuls and Hindus leading to eventual occupation of India, and the ruthless massacres during the partition of India, have left their mark on Muslim-non-Muslim relations. These relations have further deteriorated by the occupation of Muslim territories such as Palestine, Kashmir and Chechnya. The events of 9/11, invasion of Iraq, and ongoing battles between Al-Qaeda and US led military alliance have created further rift between both Muslims and non-Muslims as well as between foes and sympathizers of Al-Qaeda, Hamas, Islamic Jihad, and other militant Muslim groups (an extensive list of such militant groups is posted in the internet by the US Department of State). These events have given birth to five major entities in our time namely:

1. Jihad and Terrorism
2. War against Terrorism
3. International Military Coalition
4. The Patriot Act (USA)
5. Department of Home Land Security (USA).

The collective impact of these entities on Islam has been the departure of Islamic glories. While these glories are conspicuously visible in history and in expertly crafted marble structures such as the Taj Mahal (built by Emperor Shah Jahan), Muslim subservience can be seen throughout the Islamic world.

TAJ MAHAL

Gradual collapse of Muslim dominance, and rise of Christian and Jewish dominated political and ideological invasions have left Muslims in a state of wishful thinking as quoted in the *Encyclopedia of Islam:*

"Jihad will continue until Islam makes itself over."

This fervor has been further strengthened by improper application of Quranic verses as outlined below:

> O believers! Prepare yourself for encounter—let it be known that only those people should fight in the cause of Allah who are willing to exchange the life of this world for the Hereafter and whoever dies for the cause of Allah, whether he dies or is victorious, will soon be granted a mighty reward. (4:71-74)
>
> Those who are believers fight in the cause of Allah and those who are unbelievers fight in the cause of Taghut (forces of the devil); so fight against the helpers of Shaitan. (4:76)

Although these verses emphasize on fighting in the cause of Allah, militant Muslim groups have taken full advantage of them in their public relations campaigns, and recruitment of fedain who are brainwashed to become Shaheed (martyrs). Muslim militancy, unfortunately, has transformed the entire globe into killing fields, and the non-Muslim world has simply lost respect and trust for all Muslims. Moderate and non-militant Muslims, as well as informed non-Muslims, such as Karen Armstrong, are faced with convincing the entire world about the non-violent aspects of Islam, but no one seems to buy it privately. Publicly, however, in the interest of global diplomacy, western heads of state, most notably George Bush of the United States, have attempted to convince their citizens about the peaceful aspects of Islam as they do not want to alienate their Muslim allies. These allies have provided a strong foothold by granting either: (A) Establishment of military bases on their soil or (B) Lucrative construction projects. Their unwritten charter is to assure: (A) Uninterrupted flow of oil which is the lifeblood of the western economy, and (B) Support US efforts in the global democratization process.

History has shown that occupation of a state begins with military presence, eventually leading to a foreign rule. The

American Indians, the Hindus of India, the Muslims of the Arabian peninsula, the Christians of Greece, Sicily, and Spain, the Buddhist of Cambodia, Vietnam, Laos, Tibet, and Thailand, the Aborigines of Australia, the Zoroastrians of Iran, and many other peoples over the centuries have seen their independence, their national treasures, their economic stability, and their dignity taken away by foreign invaders. In retrospect, the anger of the militant Muslims is somewhat justified. No free Muslim or non-Muslim wants to become a pawn in the chess game of a foreign ruler, the rule be direct or indirect. The eventual outcome of this anger is mutiny, civil war, insurrection, and Jihad, all resulting in bloodshed and human suffering. What is un-Islamic in this scenario is the mode of operation of the militant Muslims and their adversaries. It is often said that "all is fair in love and war". Whoever came up with this statement was a moron and mentally deranged. It is not fair to kill innocent and defenseless human beings by flying airplanes into buildings, launching missiles on shanty camps, sending suicide bombers into cafes, sub-ways, and shopping centers, bulldozing houses of innocent people, murdering harmless contract and relief workers, killing innocent school children, and blowing up hotels and trains. It is also not fair to rape innocent women, abuse Prisoners of War (POW), and shoot to kill unarmed wounded men in a battle.

DANIEL PEARL MURDERED IN PAKISTAN (JOURNALIST)
(PHOTOGRAPH: COURTESY OF NPR.ORG)

MARGARET HASSAN MURDERED IN IRAQ
(DIRECTOR OF CARE IN IRAQ)
(PHOTOGRAPH: COURTESY OF NPR.ORG)

Human race collectively, is engaged in committing crime against humanity, be that under the pretense of Jihad, terrorism, weapons of mass destruction (WMD), or anything else. The Islamic perspective on the issue of territorial violence is quite clear, and a close scrutiny of relevant Quranic verses is a testimony of Islam's visionary attributes.

Quran allows fighting (Jihad) only in the cause of Allah and to protect the weak, oppressed old men, women, and crying children. (4:74-76)

Anyone who kills a believer intentionally will go to hell as his or her punishment. (4:93)

Quran forbids suicide; and suicide bombing of innocent people, regardless of their religious affiliation, is prohibited. (4:29)

The following Ahadith reinforce this Quranic prohibition. The Prophet (pbuh) said:

- Whoever commits suicide with a piece of iron will be punished with the same piece of iron in the Hellfire. (Narrated by Thabit-bin-Ad-Dahak)
- A man was inflicted with wounds and he committed suicide, and so Allah said: My slave has caused death on himself hurriedly, so I forbid paradise for him. (Sahih Al-Bukhari, Vol. 2 Hadith No. 45)

- He who commits suicide by throttling shall keep on throttling himself in the Hellfire, and he who commits suicide by stabbing himself shall keep on stabbing himself in the Hellfire. (Sahih Al-Bukhari Vol. 2 Hadith No. 446)

The Palestinian-Israeli conflict has given rise to suicide bombing and supporters of the Palestinian cause have quietly approved this method of retaliation. It has often been said that when one's back is against the wall, he must do anything to defend himself. This argument is understandable but not Islamic. If Palestinian men and women wish to strap bombs on their bodies and blow themselves up to kill Israelis, it is their decision. But there is nothing Islamic about this practice. They do have the right to defend themselves, but they do not have the right to defame Islam and the rest of the Muslims of the world.

Sadly speaking, mostly young men and women are brain washed to carry out this horrible act by their leaders and Imams who themselves have deviated from the Prophet's (pbuh) approach of diplomacy and peaceful resolution of conflicts. While these leaders continue to exploit the younger population, they lead a sheltered life protected by bodyguards.

A TYPICAL SUICIDE BOMBER

Militant Muslims around the globe have not succeeded in liberating their claimed land from the occupiers, and continuation of territorial violence has simply yielded no results. The repercussion of this violence has been seen in the increase in the number of widows and orphans who see no light at the end of the tunnel. Their future is doomed because their deceased fathers' and husbands' convictions to eradicate the infidel have brought nothing but death and sufferings. The perils of Taliban and Al-Qaeda initiated wars, as well as, human barbarism are well documented and cause sadness in all corners of the world.

Militant Muslims who pray for their victory need to look at the military might of countries committed to fight Arab led terrorism, most notably—the United States, Great Britain, China, Israel, India, Pakistan, Turkey, France, Russia, Germany, and others. It is no picnic to be blown away by a Hellfire missile whose lethality no Muslim knows better than me because I participated in the design and fabrication of this missile, as well as other weapon systems that exist in the arsenal of the United States, Israel, and NATO countries, who have procured these weapons under the Foreign Military Sale (FMS) and International Traffic in Arms Regulations (ITAR).

It is time for militant Muslims to put away their arms and settle their territorial disputes with prudence and diplomacy. By

EXECUTION OF A TALIBAN POW
(PHOTOGRAPH: COURTESY OF *MAGAZINE TIME*)

15 CHILDREN KILLED IN AFGHANISTAN

MILITANT MUSLIMS TERRORISE MOROCCO

VICTIMS OF TALIBAN ATROCITIES

MILITANT MUSLIMS DESTROY A SUBWAY IN MOSCOW

MUSLIM REFUGEES IN KOSOVO

MILITANT MUSLIMS STRIKE A MARRIOTT

GENOCIDE IN RWANDA

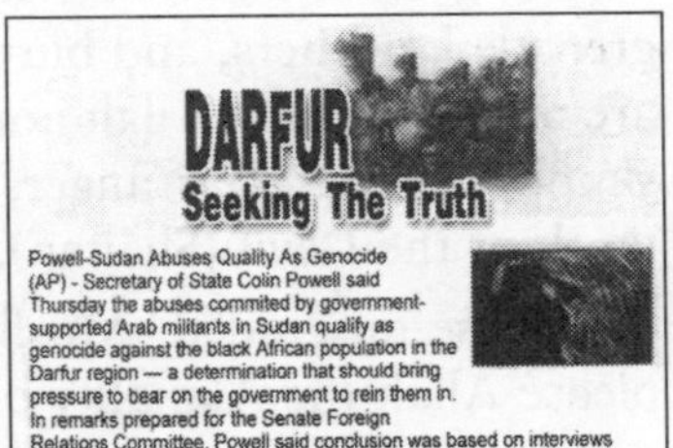

DARFUR
Seeking The Truth

Powell-Sudan Abuses Quality As Genocide (AP) - Secretary of State Colin Powell said Thursday the abuses commited by government-supported Arab militants in Sudan qualify as genocide against the black African population in the Darfur region — a determination that should bring pressure to bear on the government to rein them in. In remarks prepared for the Senate Foreign Relations Committee. Powell said conclusion was based on interviews conducted with refugees from the Darfur violence as well as other evidence

GENOCIDE IN DARFUR-SUDAN

THE VICTIMS OF HUMAN BARBARISM
(PHOTOGRAPHS: COURTESY OF *TIME MAGAZINE*)

THE ENEMIES OF PEACEFUL ISLAM
(PHOTOGRAPHS: COURTESY OF *TIME MAGAZINE*)

chanting Allahu-Akbar (Allah is great), wielding homemade grenade launchers, and burning Israeli as well as US flags, they are neither serving Allah nor the cause of their people. They are simply venting their anger, which according to Quran, is the work of the Devil (Shaitan).

These misguided Muslims must choose sides—whether to please Allah the Almighty or the devil.

Quran says:

> Whoever takes Shaitan (Devil) as a guardian instead of Allah, has indeed become a clear-cut loser. (4:119)

APACHE HELICOPTER

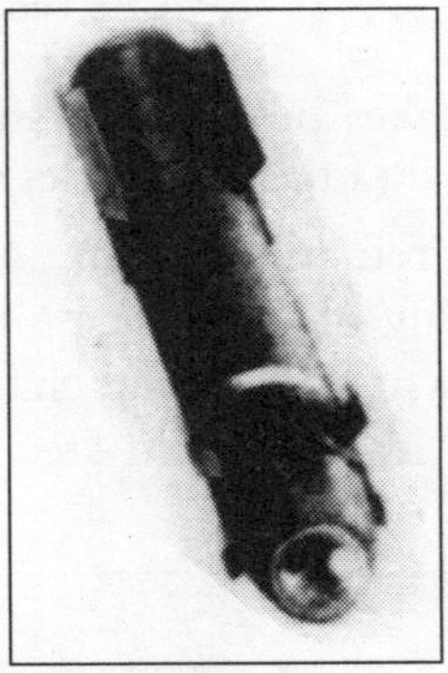

HELLFIRE

F-16 FIGHTER AIRCRAFT

THE US MILITARY MIGHT

APACHE HELICOPTER

> Shaitan makes promises to stir up in them false desires. But Shaitan makes them promises only to deceive them. (4:120)

In closing remarks, militant Muslims need to learn from the wishful thinking of the great political cynic of the Renaissance, Machiavelli, who in the final chapter of *The Prince*, contended that a strong leader would steer the decayed and fragmented

BURNING OF ISRAELI FLAG
(PHOTOGRAPH: COURTESY OF *TIME MAGAZINE*)

early sixteenth century Italy back to glory*. THIS GLORY NEVER BECAME REALITY!

BURIAL SITE OF MACHIAVELLI AND HIS DREAMS
SANTA CROCE—FLORENCE-ITALY
(PHOTOGRAPH: COURTESY OF BARNES & NOBLE BOOKS)

* *Arrogant Capital* by Kevin Phillips, p. 165, a Little Brown & Co. Publication.

Treatment of Non-Muslims in Islam

4

Muslims frequently find anti-Semitic, anti-Christian and anti-unbeliever (such as Hinduism and Buddhism) verses in the Quran (see Appendix F) and run with them to resolve crises. They often forget the circumstances under which such verses were incorporated in the Quran and fail to pay heed to verses that diffuse tension and hostilities, be that physical or ideological. A common Muslim argument or defense in support of Islam is the meaning of Islam itself—submission or surrender to the will of God. In essence, anyone who is even remotely religious is a follower of Islam because he or she submits to the commands of a deity, the definition or perception of which varies from one religion to the other. This is as far as the literal meaning of Islam takes one, because then comes the most important injunction of Islam, Shahada "La Ilaha Illallah, Muhammad-ur-Rasoolullah" [There is none but Allah who we must worship and Muhammad (pbuh) is His Rasool (Messenger)]. Shahada establishes the beginning of the Islamic monotheism which is shared by both Christians and Jews with some variations, but not by Hindus, Buddhist, and others who worship idols and practice polytheism. Although Muslims affirm the prophethood of Jesus (pbuh), Moses (pbuh) and other prophets, the divinity of Islam and the prophethood of Muhammad (pbuh) have not been revered by other arms of the hexagon (see Chapter 2).

The religious football between Islam and Christianity is thrown back and forth. Muslim scholars question the authenticity of the four Christian Gospels. Muhammad Ata-ur-Rahim and Ahmad Thomson write in their book—*Jesus Prophet of Islam:*

> Although there is some truth in them, it has been established that the four accepted gospels have not only been altered and censored through the ages, but also are not eyewitness accounts.

The authenticity of Quran has been questioned by Edward Gibbon and others as previously stated. Another sticking debate is the Unity of God in Islam and the Trinitarian Concept of God in Christianity. The architect of the Trinitarian Concept was Paul, subsequently enforced by Constantine. According to historians, movements within Christianity had divided the Christians in two groups—the Unitarians and the Paulinians. Upon the rise of Islam, reportedly a large number of Unitarian Christians, who did not support the Paulinian Doctrine of Trinity, converted to Islam. Muslims today, however, must realize that the Trinitarian Doctrine has been engraved into Christian minds since around 350 AD, and any debate on this subject is a fruitless effort. Similarly, Christians must understand that over fourteen hundred years of Islamization, will render any debate on the authenticity of Quran and prophethood of Muhammad (pbuh) useless and wasteful. Trinity is here to stay and so are Islam and Quran. *The Christian belief—Christ died for their sins, and Muslim belief that Christ was never crucified (Quran 4:157) are not going away. The Christian belief to worship Jesus and the Muslim belief that Jesus never asked to worship him except Allah (Quran 3:79) will exist till the Day of Resurrection.* Muslims and Christians may continue to throw boomerangs at each other, but they will always come back to them.

Jewish transgressions have existed since the time of the Prophet (pbuh) whose call to Dawa (acceptance of Islam) was rejected by the Jews. The Quranic verses shown in Appendix F pinpoint this Jewish transgression. The rift between Muslims and Jews has existed since the famous Hijra of the Prophet (pbuh) from Mecca to Medina (Yathrib). While the pagans of Medina supported him and accepted Islam, the Jews did not as they were well-versed in their own scriptures and religion. The first step to secede from the Jewish influence, which is a subject of Muslim pride even to this date, was the change of direction for prayer from Jerusalem to Kaaba in Mecca. This was the beginning of a deeper dissension between Muslims and Jews. History has shown that this rift further expanded when the Jews failed to support the Muslims in battles against the Meccans;

Muslims and Jews failed to live together; and subsequently, Jews were forced to leave Medina.

This chronicle of Jewish persecution by Muslims, albeit, is enough to create anti-Islamic sentiments among Jews.

CHANGE OF PRAYER DIRECTION
(PHOTOGRAPHS: COURTESY OF *TIME MAGAZINE*)

A depiction of hostilities of one community against another has always produced hard feelings. Mel Gibson's "Passion of Christ" has resulted in a subtle dislike for Jews among the Christians; Hitler's persecution of Jews has been mentioned time and time again when one wants to present an example of extreme barbarism—an act that was committed by Christian Germany. Nevertheless, Christians and Jews have now learned to live side by side. They have formed military alliance and signed treaties for mutual defense, as well as economic cooperation. The Christian-Jewish cooperation has yielded both prosperity and strength. On the contrary, the Arab-Jew conflict, mainly involving Palestine, has not only evolved into a global Muslim-Jew conflict, it has transformed the Muslim ummah into an impoverished and indignant nation. It is a shame that rather than being proud of his/her heritage, a Muslim is put in a state of hiding his/her identity and explaining to the whole world the virtues of Islam. Defenseless, spiritually bankrupt, financially destitute, and theologically closed minded are the Muslims today, and doomed to face oblivion if they do not wake up. They can, certainly, continue to follow the anti-Semitic, anti-Christian, and anti-Hindu verses of Quran, carry on their hostilities and anti-American rhetoric, but where they will end up is quite obvious. While America is rebuilding a monument to the World Trade Center on Ground Zero; the Pentagon has been completely restored; establishments, such as the Holy Land Foundation which support terrorism, are being shut down; and Muslim weapons traders are being put behind bar; Muslim nations are preparing to become pseudomorphous colonies, and amend their cultural values to comply with the wishes of the colonial powers. This transmigration of Islam into a new cultural and theological identity can be prevented if the leaders and scholars of Islam unite to bring an end to hostilities against Jews, Christians (Americans particularly), Hindus, and others. A lesson well learnt is Libya's voluntary withdrawal from production of Weapons of Mass Destruction (WMD). Muslims and the Arab World may not like it, but Libya is bound to benefit from this move without selling their Islamic values.

Dr. Al-Qaradawi* has offered his views supported with Quranic provisions that emphasize peaceful co-existence with non-Muslims and cessation of violence.

> In summary, a spiritual kinship and relationship exist between the People of the Book (Christians and Jews) and Muslims; the three religions had their roots from Abraham and foster the belief in one God and His Prophets; Muslims are allowed to eat their food; marry their women; and believe in the divinity of their Books. It is thus important to remember that Islam, Christianity and Judaism form the three arms of the hexagon (as discussed in Chapter 2) and we cannot afford the breakage of any one arm if we believe in fostering global peace and cessation of violence.

The other three arms of the hexagon, Hinduism, Buddhism, and the others, though totally divorced from Islam, Christianity, and Judaism, are equally important. In spite of the fact that Quran contains many rhetorical verses addressing or dealing with unbelievers. Quran also offers guidance when dealing with non-Muslims.

> Quran says:
>
> Allah does not forbid you to be kind and equitable to those who had neither fought against your faith nor driven you out of your homes. In fact, all loves the equitable. (60:8)
>
> O Believers! Be steadfast for the sake of Allah and bear true witness and let not the enmity of people incite you to do injustice; do justice that is nearer to piety. (5:8)

A recent Indian movie titled "Dev" has very well depicted the Hindu-Muslim hostilities which result in casualties from both sides. The root cause of the hostilities was mass ignorance and misdirected religious fervor which provided the opportunists, both Muslims and Hindus, a chance to play on the emotions of the populace and cause havoc. Granted that the Muslims of India cannot change the mindset of the Hindu majority, they can, certainly, change their own mental faculties by acquiring knowledge about Islam, and passing this knowledge to the illiterate and uneducated Muslims.

---

* *The Lawful and Prohibited in Islam.*

A Hadith of the Prophet (pbuh) reported by Al-Bukhari emphasizes the importance of gaining knowledge. A summary of this Hadith is as follows:

> The Prophet (pbuh) said once that knowledge is synonymous to abundant rain that falls on the earth; some of this rain falls on fertile soil and produces vegetation and grass; some falls on hard ground and is held which both people and animals drink; and some falls on barren land which could neither hold water nor produce vegetation; the person who does not care to gain knowledge and seek Allah's guidance is like the barren waste land. (Sahih Al-Bukhari, Hadith #70, pp. 88-89)

The above Hadith is strengthened by Quran.

> Quran says:
>
> The good soil yields rich produce by permission of Allah and barren soil yields nothing but poor produce. (7:58)
>
> The worst animals in the sight of Allah are those deaf and dumb people who do not use common sense. (8:122)
>
> And those who reject the truth and do not become believers. (5:55)

In another Hadith narrated by Abu Huraira, the Prophet (pbuh), in response to a tribesman's question regarding the Doomsday said:

> When the power or authority comes in the hands of unfit persons, then wait for the Doomsday. (Sahih Al-Bukhari)

The hypocrisy of radical Muslims, politicians, and clergymen (Mullas, Ayatollas, and clerics) is very well addressed in Quran.

> Quran says:
>
> Among the people there is one whose speech fascinates you in this worldly life, he may even call upon Allah to witness what is in his heart, yet he is your staunch opponent. (2:204)
>
> And when he leaves you, he directs his efforts towards causing mischief in the land, destroying crops and cattle. (2:205)
>
> *Note:* Crops and Cattle in 2:205 are allegorical and simply focus one's attention to overall destruction.

The above Quranic verses and Ahadith send a powerful message to both Muslims and non-Muslims. A need for acquiring knowledge, and channeling this knowledge for the good of mankind, therefore, becomes the responsibility of every Muslim and non-Muslim. Only when both Muslims and non-Muslims would carry the zeal to benefit the community, and understand the Prophet's (pbuh) concept of Rahma, they will be able to steer the community in the direction of peace, and peaceful co-existence with one another. It will prevent self-serving politicians, pundits and mullahs from leading the population in the path of destruction and bloodshed. Muslims of India must understand that Hinduism is here to stay, and forms one of the important arms of the religious hexagon. History has shown that Muslim scholars have preferred benevolent non-Muslim rulers over barbaric Muslim rulers who, in the name of Islam, carry on atrocities that would put Islam to shame.*

Yes, the Hindus are infidels or Kafirs. So what? Do Quran, Bible, and Torah predict the coming of another prophet who will eradicate idol worship? Is another Muawiya or Saladdin Ghazi coming to restore lost Islamic glories by driving Hindus into the Indian Ocean? Is another Qaede-Azam (great leader) descending from the heavens to partition India once again and create Pakistan 2? The answers of these questions are "definitely not". Let this be a wake up call for those Muslims who have thrived on the ignorance of the innocent masses and exploited them under the banner of Islam. *ASIDE FROM SELF-DEFENSE, THERE IS NOTHING ISLAMIC ABOUT VIOLENCE.* In the words of Malcolm X:

> There is nothing in our book Koran that teaches us to suffer peacefully. Our religion teaches us to be intelligent, be peaceful, be courteous, obey the law, respect everyone, but if someone puts his hand on you, send him to the cemetery, that is good religion.
>
> (Published in *Malcolm X Speaks)*

The Prophet (pbuh), in his lifetime, made it mandatory that non-Muslim citizens (known as DHIMMIS then) are well protected

---

* *The Political Language of Islam* by Bernard Lewis, p. 107, a University of Chicago Press Publication.

and no harm came to them. There are several Ahadith on this subject as shown below:*

The Prophet (pbuh) said:

- He who hurts Dhimmis hurts me and annoys Allah.
- Whoever hurts Dhimmis, I am his adversary, and I shall be an adversary to him on the Day of Resurrection.

  On the Day of Resurrection, I shall dispute with anyone who oppresses a person from among the People of the Covenant, or infringes on his rights, or put a responsibility on him which is beyond his strength, or takes something from him against his will.

After the death of the Prophet (pbuh), his successors carried on the convictions of the Prophet (pbuh), and safeguarded the rights and sanctity of the non-Muslim citizens. Two prominent jurists of Islam have expressed their views on the rights of non-Muslims as shown below:

*The Maliki Jurist—Shah al-Deen al-Qarafi**

The covenant of protection imposes upon us certain obligations toward the Ahl Al-Dhimmah (Non-Muslims). They are our neighbors, under our shelter, and protection upon the guarantee of Allah, His Messenger (pbuh), and the religion of Islam. Whoever violates these obligations against anyone of them by so much as an abusive word, by slandering his reputation, or by doing him some injury, or assisting in it, has breached the guarantee of Allah, His Messenger (pbuh), and the religion of Islam.

The Zahiri Jurist—Ibn Hazm

If one is a Dhimmi, and the enemy comes with his forces to take him, it is our obligation to fight the enemy with soldiers and weapons, and to give our lives for him, thus honoring Allah and His Messenger (pbuh).

The above Ahadith and views of the jurists further strengthen the hexagon concept, and reinforce the belief in peaceful coexistence with other arms of the hexagon.

---

* *The Lawful and Prohibited in Islam.*

Unfortunately, the militancy of a handful of fanatical Muslims led by individuals, such as Osama-bin-Laden and Al-Zarqawi, and groups, such as Hamas, Ansar-al-Islam, Islamic Jihad etc., has put Islam on a direct collision course with international intuitionalism, and threatens to disintegrate the hexagon. The damage that this militancy has done to peace loving Muslims is insurmountable, just to mention a few:

- All mosques are classified as breeding grounds for terrorists.
- All Muslims living in the West as well as those who visit them go through excessive surveillance routinely.
- Most Muslim institutions are aligned with Holy Land Foundation, and are considered as a threat to homeland security.

Who is to blame—USA, the Western Alliance, or the nations who have taken a vow to eradicate Islamic fanaticism, and drive out militant Muslim groups from their land? No, the blame lies on the few Muslim militants who have inflicted humiliation upon all Muslims. Their martyrdom is merely a mirage that has not even put a dent in the military might of the coalition led by USA.

Yes their suicide bombers and car bombs have caused some destruction, but achieved nothing else. When the Imam of Albany, New York mosque negotiates for shoulder fired missiles within the premises of the mosque, the Scotland Yard finds a stockpile of chemical weapons protective gear in a London, England mosque, and insurgents operate from the Mother of All Battles Mosque in Iraq, which Muslim, in his right might, would say that the West is unjust in labeling mosques as the breeding grounds for terrorists? Quran, in several verses, has admonished these enemies of Islam who call themselves Muslims:

> Quran says:
>
> There are those who built a Masjid (mosque) (Masjid-e-Zirar) for mischievous motives to spread disbelief and to disunite the believers—they will indeed swear that their intentions are nothing but good, but Allah declares that they are absolute liars. (9:107)

> Certainly, the Masjid founded on piety is more deserving—for in it there are men (and women) who love to be purified; and Allah loves those who purify themselves. (9:108)
>
> Who is a better person, he who lays the foundation of his building on piety to Allah and His good pleasure, or he who lays the foundation of his building on an undermined bank that will tumble down with him in the fire of Hell. Allah does not guide such wrong doers. (9:109)

The loud and clear message to both Muslims and Islam bashers, in the light of the above Quranic verses, is:

> ISLAM AND QURAN DO NOT SUPPORT CONVERSION OF PLACES OF WORSHIP (MOSQUES) INTO (A) STORAGE FACILITIES FOR WEAPONS, AND (B) FORTRESSES FROM WHERE BATTLES CAN BE FOUGHT.

It is the duty of all living and breathing Muslims to see that their mosques do not become Masjid-e-Zirar.

The Muslim clergy today prays for the victory of Muslims in Kashmir, Palestine, Chechnya, and elsewhere in the world. Rarely anyone prays for world peace and inculcation of the Prophet's (pbuh) concept of Rahma to resolve crises. Quran has repeatedly mentioned destruction of the people of other prophets *(7:64, 7:72, 7:78, 7:84, 7:91, 7:130, 11:60, 11:67, 11:82, 11:89, 11:94, 11:109, 23:44, 26:120, 26:172, 29:38, 36:29, 40:78, 51:38-46, 54:31, 54:34)* and arrival of new prophets to guide the nations left behind by the previous prophets *(10:47, 10:74, 13:7, 37:171)*. Since Muhammad (pbuh) is the last prophet according to Sunni Muslim belief, and no Imami Shia knows when the Mehdi will arrive from hiding to set the world straight, who is around to protect the Muslims from destruction today? The absence of a future prophet or an Imam, undoubtedly, puts the burden on bearded, black robed, turban clad Mullahs and Ayatollas, as well as on clean shaven, tailored suit clad, American cigarette/Cuban cigar smoking secularists, who must get out of their sheltered life in Qum, Najaf, Mecca, Riyadh, Cairo, Damascus, Rawalpindi, Islamabad, New Delhi, Kolkata, Istanbul, Ankara, Dhaka, Lagos, Tripoli, Kabul, Jakarta, Chicago, New York, Houston, Atlanta, Toronto, and elsewhere in the world to prevent destruction of the Muslim ummah. The burden also lies on every adult Muslim man and woman who must carry the banner of Islam with utmost piety and sincerity, keeping the welfare of both Muslims and non-Muslims as their prime priority, while maintaining a realistic Islamic way of life. A realistic Islamic way of life is simply a lifestyle which is not marred with exaggerations, misinterpretations, moral bankruptcy, defunct spiritualism, lack of patience and perseverance, indecency, bias, debilitating compassion for humanity, and an exponential rise in violence under the pretense of Jihad. Muslims must live up to the injunction of Quran.

Quran says:

> You (Muslims) are the best nation which has ever been raised for the guidance of mankind. You enjoin good, forbid evil, and believe in Allah. (3:110)

The responsibility to show the rest of the world that Muslims are the best nation, lies on every Muslim.

IS ISLAM A RELIGION OF PEACE OR VIOLENCE?

Any discussion on Islam will be regarded as biased if the non-conciliatory or inflammatory verses of Quran are not discussed, and a proper explanation of these verses is not offered to alleviate the dichotomy. On one hand Muslims portray Islam to be a religion of peace, and on the other hand, it (Islam) propagates anti-Semitic, anti-Christian, and anti-Infidel sentiments through Quranic verses. A reader gets confused and simply asks "What is going on? Is Islam a religion of peace or hate and violence against non-Muslims?"

This discussion, though complex, must be undertaken with objectivity and open-mindedness.

In many verses, Quran addresses transgression by Jews, and the ultimate punishment that they will receive on the Day of Resurrection. This subject must be viewed in historical prospective. Judaism existed prior to the coming of Islam and Christianity. Jewish behavior in early biblical and Islamic times has been anything but compassionate and conciliatory. "PASSION OF CHRIST" has depicted the Jewish mentality against Christ, and Quran has presented Muhammad's (pbuh) frustrations with Jews because of their lack of co-operation and betrayal. As discussed earlier, Jews neither embraced

Muhammad's (pbuh) message nor supported the Muslims in battles against the pagans of Arabia. Consequently, "Jewish Transgression" became the seal of Muslim anathema. In retrospect, had the Jews accepted the Prophet's (pbuh) message and embraced Islam, anti-Semitism would have simply vanished from all Islamic scriptures.

In the twenty-first century, anti-Semitism has proven to be fatal, not only for the Arabs who share their borders with the only Jewish state, Israel, but for the entire Muslim ummah. The Palestinian-Israeli conflict has further added fuel to the fire, and led to global violence labeled as "Islamic Terrorism". Realistically speaking, if a society refuses to accept a new philosophy, be that political or religious, the instigator of the new philosophy should either manage the conflict with wisdom and compassion, or leave them alone to practice their belief, as the Prophet (pbuh) did. But no, we expect the entire world population to conform to our ideals, and when that does not materialize, we label the non-compliant population as Transgressors, Insurgents, Terrorists, Infidels, Atankwadis, and so on. The transgressors are punished in the scriptures, and the others are punished with military alliances. Muslims can, certainly, continue the doctrine of hate, but they have much to lose and little to gain. The transgressors (Jews, Christians, Hindus etc.) can no longer be driven into the oceans, and this is the reality that Muslims, Arabs particularly, cannot swallow. Granted that the Prophet (pbuh) had his differences with the Jews, and was deeply hurt by their betrayal, but he, subsequently, adopted a highly pragmatic approach to unity. Not only he was a messenger of God, he was a prudent and compassionate statesman and leader who cared for the welfare of both Muslims and non-Muslims.

As we have seen before, Imams, such as Al-Bukhari, Muslims, and others have painstakingly collected the Prophet's (pbuh) statements and rulings and combined them in the form of Ahadith which shape the daily life of a believing Muslim. An integral part of this belief is to refrain from extremism. In one Hadith reported by Abu Huraira, the Prophet (pbuh) said:

> Religion is very easy, and whoever overburdens himself in his religion, will not be able to continue in that way. So you should not be extremist. (Sahih Al-Bukhari)

In another Hadith, reported by Abu Huraira,

> The Prophet (pbuh) prayed for the guidance of the Al-Mushrikun (the polytheists, idol worshippers, etc.). (Al-Bukhari)

At this point, it would be prudent to address the question—what has gone wrong with Islam in the context of global terrorism and violence by Muslims. As the above Hadith states, a small segment of the Muslim population, mostly Arabs and their sympathizers, have resorted to extremism whose foundation is distortion and aberration. The principal culprit in this scenario is perverted Wahabism, the doctrine followed by Osama-bin-Laden, his Al-Qaeda organization, and Saudi religious establishments. As Muslims around the globe, Sunnis in particular, look up to Saudi Arabia in matters of religion, any edict or verdict that prevails there, is easily exported by Islamic zealots regardless of its merits or flaws. The virtues of Wahabism, as introduced by Abdal Wahab in the eighteenth century in Najf, has been transformed, from a doctrine based on a strictly literal interpretation of Quran and the Sunnah, to a doctrine that promotes hate and violence. To make matters worst, a number of Muslim scholars most notably Ahmad Taha of Egypt, Mir Hamza of Pakistan, and Fazlur Rahman of Bangladesh, have supported this extremist view and Jihad against the United States.*

In theirs as well as Osama-bin-Laden's mind, they are engaged in the eighth crusade which will cease when Muslim glories are restored—a Machiavellian wish! Natana, in her book, writes:

> Some westerners envision Wahabism as a creed that promotes extremism and fanatical discourse combined with violence and intolerant tendencies.

This statement is highly offensive, and a slap on all Wahabis. Wahabism in itself does not promote violence. It is the misinterpretations and misapplications of the Quranic provisions of which Osama-bin-Laden and other militant Muslims, in the

---

* *Wahabi Islam* by Natana J. Delong-Bas, published by Oxford University Press.

name of Islam, are taking advantage. Wahabism contains all the elements of self-purification and the Prophet's (pbuh) approach to life's issues without entertaining violence and intolerance.

Another partner in crime is Ayaman Al-Zawahiri, a major Sufi. As we recall, Sufism fosters an approach to Islam based on personal piety and tolerance with local traditions. This marriage of inappropriate Wahabism, and distorted Sufism is quite puzzling. Nevertheless, the readers must understand that neither Wahabism nor Sufism condone violence. *WHAT IS GOING ON IS TOTALLY UN-ISLAMIC*. We can only pray and convey the true message of Islam hoping for the demise of radicalism, and defamation of Islam caused by a handful of misguided Muslims.

Western analysts, such as Lisa Bayer of *Time Magazine* and John Esposito of Georgetown University (USA), have attempted to analyze the sources of Muslim militancy and hatred towards the United States. A summary of their analysis alludes to the following conclusion:

> The present hostility of militant Muslims, mostly Arabs, can be directed to one major source—US foreign policy—unequivocal support of Israel, sanctions against Muslim countries, invasion of Iraq, vetoing most anti-Israeli resolutions in the United Nations, and other military interventions. This policy has given the Muslims a bad taste in the mouth as John Esposito says: *"Many Arabs and Muslims feel impotent. Their sense of identity is wounded."* While Esposito's choice of the word "impotent" reveals inappropriateness of his mental faculties, and could irritate any Muslim, it does point to an ailment which has inflicted the Muslim ummah—a diversion from Islam. An ailment, nevertheless, requires the services of a qualified physician, who prescribes the proper medication. The cure for the Muslim ailment is not terrorism and violence. The prescription was revealed to the Prophet (pbuh) in the cave of Hera, the Quran. As an improper use or application of a medication causes a fatal injury, Arabs and Muslims will prolong their ailment if they continue to engage in distortion of Quranic verses and justify their adversarial role under the shadow of Jihad.

Karen Armstrong, in a *Time Magazine* article published on October 1, 2001 writes:

> It would be as grave a mistake to see Osama-bin-Laden as an authentic representative of Islam as to consider James Kopp, the alleged killer of an abortion provider in Buffalo, N.Y., a typical Christian or Baruch Goldstein, who shot 29 worshippers in the Hebron mosque in 1994 and died in the attack, a true martyr of Israel. The vast majority of Muslims, who are horrified by the atrocity of Sept. 11, must reclaim their faith from those who have so violently hijacked it.

(May the Lord bless her with long life!)

Muslims must understand that all human beings live by some codes of conduct which prevent them from becoming animals. It is totally acceptable to enlighten non-Muslims, and convey the message of Islam, because only then they will respect Islam and its virtues. This, however, cannot be achieved with the Lion King mentality, as a lion, without claws and teeth, is just another pussy cat.

A LION OR A PUSSY CAT?
(PHOTOGRAPH: COURTESY OF REVIEW AND HERALD)

APPENDIX F

NON-CONCILIATORY VERSES OF QURAN

Verse	Quran Says
AL-BAQARAH	
2:51	A wicked transgression by Israelites who took the calf for worship.
2:59	But the wrong doers (Israelites) changed our words (instead of saying "we repent") from that which they were asked to say, so We sent down a scourge from heavens as a punishment for their transgression.
2:61	Gradually they (Israelites) became so degraded that shame and misery were brought upon them.
2:64	It was the consequence of their disobedience and transgression.
2:75	Hold firmly to what We have given you (Torah) and follow the commandment therein—But even after that you backed out—you surely would have been the losers. Do you, O Believers (Muslims), still hope that they (People of the Book) will believe in what you say, when some of them have already perverted it knowingly after they understood it.
2:80	The Jews say: "The fire shall not touch us except for a few days—those (Jews) who commit evil became encircled in sin are inmate of Hellfire.
2:83	Remember, we took a covenant from the children of Israel but you (Jews) broke the covenant.
2:90	Ridiculous is the price for which they (Jews) have sold away their soul—they have drawn upon themselves wrath upon wrath, and for such disbelievers, there is a disgraceful punishment.

Contd...

Verse	Quran Says
2:96	You will find them (Jews) the greediest of men of life, even greedier than the Mushrikun (unbelievers).
2:100	Has it not been the case that every time they made a covenant, a group of them threw it aside? But the fact is that most of them (Jews) are faithless.
2:109	Many among the People of the Book wish they could somehow turn you back to unbelief—forgive them and bear with them until Allah brings about His decision.
2:111	They say: "None shall enter the paradise except the one who is a Jew or a Christian." These are the vein desires.
2:120	The Jews and Christians will never be pleased with you until you follow their faith.
2:135	Jews and Christians say: "Be Jews or Christians", you shall then be rightly guided.
3:24	In their religion (Judaism) they are deceived by their own self-invented beliefs.
3:54	The unbelievers among the children of Israel plotted against Isa (Jesus).
3:77	Verily! Those (Jews and Christians) who sell Allah's covenant and their own oath for a petty price, shall have no portion in the hereafter. They shall have painful punishment.
3:99	Say: "O People of the Book! Why do you obstruct the believers (Muslims) in the path of Allah and desire that they follow your crooked way while you yourselves are witness to Allah's covenant? Allah is not unmindful for what you do.

Women in Islam

5

One evening, I reached the local mosque a bit early. A stocky Middle Eastern man, who had dyed his hair and beard, was discussing the reward of being a good Muslim. He went on to say "At the lowest level of the paradise, a man will be rewarded with eighty wives and eighty thousand servants." The thought immediately came to my mind that, if on the Day of Judgment, every man and woman will be judged and rewarded according

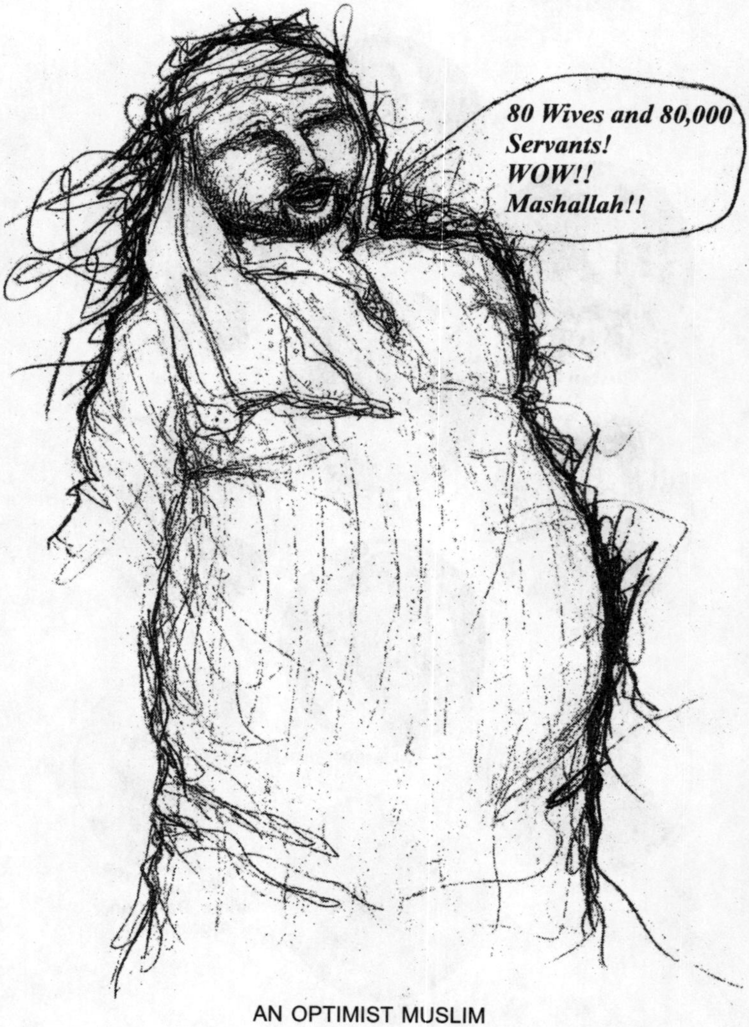

AN OPTIMIST MUSLIM

to his/her deeds, what is the reward for women. This is really a subject that requires in-depth discussion as the pride of Muslim men, and prejudices of Western news media, have presented a distorted picture of Islam in this arena. Every effort will be made to be as concise as possible.

Incidentally, Quran, in verses *52:20, 56:22, and 78:33*, does mention *"Hûr" (fair females) as well as "maidens of equal age"* who will be wives of pious men as their reward for good deeds, but neither mentions a number (80 or otherwise) nor refers to the word Virgins as heard on air waves in the US and elsewhere.

WOMEN'S RIGHTS

EQUALITY

When it comes to reward, Quran is very explicit about equality.

Quran says:

> I* will not let the good deeds of any among you go to waste be he a man or a woman. I will forgive them their sins and admit them into gardens beneath which the rivers flow. (3:95)
>
> But those who believe and do good deeds, We** shall admit them into gardens with streams of running water where they will abide for ever with fairest companions and coolest shades. (4:57)
>
> Verily men and women…those men and women who remember God a great deal, for them God has forgiveness and a great reward. (33:35)

The above verses depict that equality of men and women existed from the days of the prophet (pbuh). Ironically, however, professor Elshtain in her book titled *Just War Against Terror*, (quoting a *Time Magazine* article by Lisa Beyer) writes:

> Nowhere in the Muslim world are women treated as equals. Part of the problem dates to Muhammad. Even as he

---

* 'I' here implies God (Allah).

** 'We' here implies God (Allah).

> proclaimed new rights for women, he enshrined their inequality in immutable law, passed down as God's commandments and eventually recorded in the scripture. The Quran allots daughters half the inheritance of sons under sharia or Muslim law, the compensation for the murder of a woman is half the going rate for men. This presents enormous challenges to reformers.

Both professor Elshtain and Lisa Beyer are correct in their observation of inequality of women in Islam. Nevertheless, professor Elshtain's piecemeal observation has failed to address a very important element. In over two hundred years of democratic rule in the United States, politicians, theocrats, and academics have not been able to enforce Equal Rights Amendment which failed in 1982, and female inequality exists in many forms.

In fact, female inequality has existed in the western societies since biblical times and several verses of Bible are testimonies of this inequality as shown below:*

Exodus 20:17: States the famous tenth commandment, lumps a wife together with his servants, animals and house.

Exodus 21:7-11: A man could sell his daughter as a slave or give her in marriage to whomsoever he chose.

Leviticus 12:1-8: After the birth of a male child, a woman is ritually impure for seven days, however after the birth of a female child she is ritually impure for fourteen days according to the law of the Bible.

Corinthians 14:34-35 of the New Testament of the Bible: States that a woman should be subordinate—for it is shameful for a woman to speak in church.

Timothy 2:11: States: "Let a woman learn in silence with all submissiveness. I permit no woman to teach or have authority over men."

---

* 'Islam and Women', by Muhammed Asadi, an Internet article published in www.bigissueground.com

> According to a *New York Times* report published on October 25, 2005, under the direction of the leaders of the Fundamentalist Church of Jesus Christ of Latter Day Saints, marriages are being annulled in order to remove women from their husbands and assign them to other men, and girls under 18 are ordered to become brides of older men on a day's notice, in Arizona and Utah.

Muhammad's (pbuh) achievements, in his twenty-three lifespan as a prophet, cannot be challenged by anyone. Transformation of a pagan Arab society, which believed in female infanticide, into a new generation of God-fearing Muslims, who protected their women and compensated them, no matter how disproportionate, is a miracle that is within the comprehension of a few western women. Lisa Beyer in her *Time Magazine* article writes:

> For his day, Prophet Muhammad was a feminist. The doctrine he laid out as the revealed Word of God considerably improved the status of women in 7th century Arabia. He was a liberal at home as well as in pulpit.

Lisa Beyer's observations in the male chauvinistic practices that have caused both physical and emotional trauma to Muslim women, are understandable but not Islamic. If we look at the global picture, men of all creeds and religions have deviated from an established system of spiritual jurisprudence over the centuries. Muslims are being singled out because this is a hot topic today, and any adverse propaganda against Muslims and Islam sells to the gratification of the author. The journalistic aptitude of Professor Elshtain, and others like her, can be compared with a poker player who only shows one side of the card to raise the bet.

Benazir Bhutto (the former Prime Minister of Pakistan) and Khalida Zia (the current Prime Minister of Bangladesh) are also Muslim women, and just about in every-corner of the globe, one will find a Muslim female physician. My two daughters are also physicians and they are also Muslim women. None of these women is a victim of inequality or male chauvinism.

KHALIDA ZIA
(PRIME MINISTER)

BENAZIR BHUTTO
(FORMER PRIME MINISTER)

(PHOTOGRAPHS: COURTESY OF THE SOUTH-EAST ASIA.COM)

Although the entire world seems to be embracing the Western cultural see-saw, a concept that promotes total conformance to and acceptance of American and Western values, as they relate to women, is not the panacea for the uplift of Muslim women, simply because such a concept has its own flaws. A reform in Islam is, certainly, needed to further improve the status of women. Muslim rulers and clergy need to look beyond their personal agenda with regard to eliminating the inequality among men and women, while maintaining a socially, spiritually, and intellectually healthy Muslim ummah. A radical change is neither needed nor desired. An uplift of women needs to be every Muslim's concern, not necessarily to appease western critics, but to better the lives of Muslim women who are the breeders of the future generations. An educated, healthy, emotionally stable, and God-fearing woman is more apt to raise a child who grows up with the same values. The by-product of an uneducated, humiliated, emotionally crushed, subservient, and misguided woman is going to have similar characteristics. There is a choice to make, be that for or against reform. Muslims, therefore, must either prepare their women for the next millennium, or be doomed.

INHERITANCE

Women have a share in what parents and relatives leave behind.

Quran says:

> There is a share for men and a share for women from what is left by parents and those nearest related, whether the property be small or large—a legal share. (4:17)

DOWRY (MEHR)

Married women are entitled to a pre-negotiated dowry (Mehr). This is true even when a man divorces a woman.

Quran says:

> So with those of whom you have enjoyed, give them their Mehr as prescribed, you agree mutually. (4:25)
>
> Wed them with the permission of their own folk and give them their Mehr according to what is reasonable. (4:25)

EARNINGS

Women have a share in what they earn.

Quran says:

> For men there is a reward for what they have earned, for women there is reward for what they have earned. (4:32)

CHOOSE A HUSBAND

Both Quran and Hadith are silent on this subject except in verse 4:19.

Quran says:

> O you who believe! You are forbidden to inherit women against their will. (4:19)

The literal meaning of "inherit" is to receive or obtain by descent from an ancestor. Scholars of Islam may have their own interpretation. Nevertheless, in our time, the question of inheriting a woman does not arise. It may even be construed as slavery which is illegal just about in all countries. What is important in the above verse is "against their will". In Islam, women do have the right to choose their husbands so long as they are believing men (Muslims) and reject those who are thrust upon them by their parents and guardians against their will. This opinion is shared by Muslim scholars such as Dr. Al-Qaradawi, a detailed discussion of which is presented in Chapter 6.

The union of two incompatible individuals on the premise that love, affection, compassion, and understanding will automatically develop after marriage, has produced disastrous results and many divorces.

SEEK DIVORCE

While it is commonly believed that a man can divorce his wife by simply uttering "I divorce you" three times, a woman is not entitled to initiate a divorce. Although this subject will be addressed in greater details in Chapter 7, women do have the right to get out of a miserable marriage by a Quranic provision called Al-Khula. Khula is a process in which a wife seeks divorce from her husband by returning the Mehr (dowry) if the husband has paid it. It may also include other compensations as mutually agreed on.

CONSTITUTIONAL RIGHTS

The constitution of every country in the twenty-first century guarantees certain rights to its citizens. Women enjoy the same rights as men which are the right to vote, right to choose a profession, right to free speech etc. Observance of a country's laws is favored by Islam so long as these laws do not interfere with the canonical aspects of Islam. Traditionalists, whose life rotates around orthodoxy, may not approve certain laws, but the reality is that their traditionalism cannot supersede the laws of a country, Islamic or otherwise. A typical scenario is beating women as stated in the Quran.

Quran says:

> As to those women on whose part you see ill-conduct, admonish them (first), refuse to share their beds (next), and beat them (last). (4:34)

Beating women may have been practiced in the Prophet's (pbuh) time as a punishment for ill-conduct, cells of a jail will be decorated for those Muslim men who dare do this in our time. It is called spousal abuse and battery in the United States and elsewhere. Muslim men, for the respect of Quran, must resort to the first two provisions of verse 4:34, and must not humiliate Quran by beating their spouses. It is not going to reserve a place for them in the heavens! Furthermore, the Prophet (pbuh) disapproved beating and the pertinent Ahadith will be discussed in Chapter 7.

Another controversial issue is the nature of the punishment of a woman guilty of adultery (illegal sexual act).

Quran says:

> And those of your women who commit illegal sexual intercourse, take the evidence of four witnesses from amongst you against them, and if they testify (find her guilty), confine them to houses until death comes to them or Allah ordains for them some way. (4:15)

The confinement stated in Quran is equivalent to house arrest and most laws today do not support such "confinement till death".

Quran in verse 24:2 ordains a different punishment as stated below:

Quran says:

> The fornicatoress and the fornicator, flog each of them with a hundred stripes (lashes)—and let a party of believers witness their punishment. (24:2)

NOWHERE IN QURAN, THE PUNISHMENT FOR ADULTERY IS STONING TO DEATH. Nevertheless, hard-line Muslim scholars have cited two Ahadith for harsher punishments:

(a) An unmarried person (women or man) be exiled for one year and also receive the legal punishment *i.e.* One hundred lashes.

(b) A married person (woman or a man) be stoned to death by other Muslims.

Scholars of Islam have suggested that the provision of confinement in 4:15 has been abrogated by the provisions of 24:2. A layman might question "why is this abrogation not the other way round?" A logical answer is that verse 4:15 was revealed to the Prophet (pbuh) before verse 24:2 and, therefore, the supersession is justified.

Granted that purification of the ills of a community is tantamount to the maintenance of the canonical and spiritual values, exhibition of such extreme cruelty *i.e.* stoning of a human being to death is not supported by Quran and, therefore, the provision of the Hadith should be revisited by Muslim scholars who have, interestingly enough, devised a means to get around the prohibition of Riba (usury-interest) in Quran by introducing the concepts of *Mubashara, Ijara,* and *Mubahad* in financial transactions. They have realized that interest is an integral part of the global economy. If these scholars believe in the supremacy of Allah as well as His power to ordain some way for sinners, and are capable of getting around prohibitions in Quran, I am sure they can come up with a ruling that will stop the punishment of ending one's life by stoning.

WOMEN'S ISSUES IN THE 21ST CENTURY

SEGREGATION

Hard line Islamic traditionalism is very well presented by Milse Ruthven*. He writes about the attitude of a well respected scholar of Islam, Maulana Maududi:

> His traditionalism is most evident in his general attitude to women, and in particular, in his defense of Purdah, the complete veiling and segregation of women as practiced in India. He concludes, with impeccable logic, that women should be completely covered outside the home (where they should always remain except when absolutely necessary) because the face is the most attractive part of the human body!

Maulana Maududi's views had a cancerous effect on the followers of Islam. They have actively imposed segregation globally including the United States. This segregation has pretty much transformed Muslim communities into patriarchal societies. Women must bear their children, play a dominant role in running

---

* *Islam in the World* by Milse Ruthven.

the family, and stretch themselves in multiple directions. But socially, the majority of them continue to live as second class human beings. This is a pathetic diversion from Islamic provisions. Neither the Quran nor the Hadith condones suppression of women by men. Muslim men must provide their wives and daughters opportunities to develop into physically, intellectually, emotionally, and educationally sound members of the Islamic ummah, while inculcating in them spiritualism and Islamic values. The myopic vision of Maududi's followers allows them to see nothing beyond their orthodox dogma. They have failed to realize that women are making enormous contributions in all walks of life. In today's technologically advanced society, it has become a necessity that women stand on their own two feet. In the event of a family crisis, such as divorce or death of the bread earner, hardly anyone comes forward to help a destitute woman, Muslim or non-Muslim, who has been left with no financial support or whose assets have been devoured by greedy relatives. I have personally witnessed the horrible living conditions of several Muslim widows whose husbands did not or could not leave behind much for them to go on. Some of these women had to resort to menial jobs and subtle begging. Matrimonial websites are full of Muslim women who are literally begging Muslim men to marry them. What advice Muslim scholars have for such women? Muslim scholars, who are adamant about enforcing female segregation, need to ask themselves: "Do they want their wives and daughters become destitute and glorified beggars after they are gone?" Perhaps, they are not concerned about their own family, because the proceeds from their books, CDs, and royalties will be enough to support their wives and children. It is the ordinary Muslim women who must bear the wrath of segregation, and live a life full of humiliation and indignation. The message to these scholars and Muslim men is:

> Back off and get real; Muslim women of the twenty-first century are as capable as you are; quit your suppression and male chauvinism; stop justifying your urge to control them by corrupting Quranic verses and Ahadith; refrain from challenging their decency and morality just because they are out making a living, and contributing to the family budget; do not identify them as sex symbols which will attract every man on the street; before you throw stone at a woman, look at your own character,

morality, and convictions to piety; when a woman's beauty causes activation of your sensory nerves, and throws you in a world of fantasy, thank Allah for creating such beauty, and work harder to please Him; He may reward you with this beauty for your good deeds in this life or on the Day of Resurrection.

PRAYER OF A MUSLIM MAN

SEGREGATION AND VEILING IN HISTORY, QURAN, AND AHADITH

History

Segregation of women by Muslim men was a practice they had adopted from Greek Christians of Byzantium after the death of the Prophet (pbuh). The segregation by the Greek Christians, was a symbol of distinction between upper and lower class. It was not meant to segregate them from all men*. Although this practice has been abandoned by them, orthodox Muslims continue to put undue emphasis on it. Recent protests in France

---

* *Islam* by Karen Armstrong.

against the abolishment of veil (hijab) worn by Muslim women have revealed the rigidity of Muslim orthodoxy.

Quran

Quran says:

> And when you ask [wives of the prophet (pbuh)] for anything you want, ask them from behind a screen. (33:53)

The above verse only addresses some degree of segregation and veiling of the Prophet's (pbuh) wives. There is nothing in Quran that requires complete segregation and head-to-toe veiling of all women. In fact the women of the first ummah had taken part in public life, and fought alongside men in battle.

Quran says:

> Tell the believing women to lower their eyes, guard their private parts, and not display their charm except what is apparent outwardly, and cover their bosom with their veil and not show their finery. (24:31)
>
> And as for women past child-bearing who do not expect wedlock, it is no sin on them if they discard their (outer) clothing in such a way as not to show their adornment. (24:60)

Hadith

In one Hadith, the Prophet (pbuh) is said to have told his followers that they could learn half the religion from his wife Aisha. In another Hadith, the Prophet (pbuh) is said to have praised women who fought alongside him.

As it is apparent from the above provisions of Quran and Hadith, complete segregation and veiling of women including Maududi's cry for Purdah* and Burqa** are not justifiable. The world has seen the perils of segregation which caused the death of several Saudi female students when their school caught fire, and they could not get out because their dress did not conform to the standards of Saudi police. They were kept locked up in a blazing building.

---

* Purdah is a concept of segregation which does not allow women to come in contact of men except relatives.

** Burqa is an outer garment that covers a woman from head-to-toe with a screen or holes for eyes (see the photograph on p. 109).

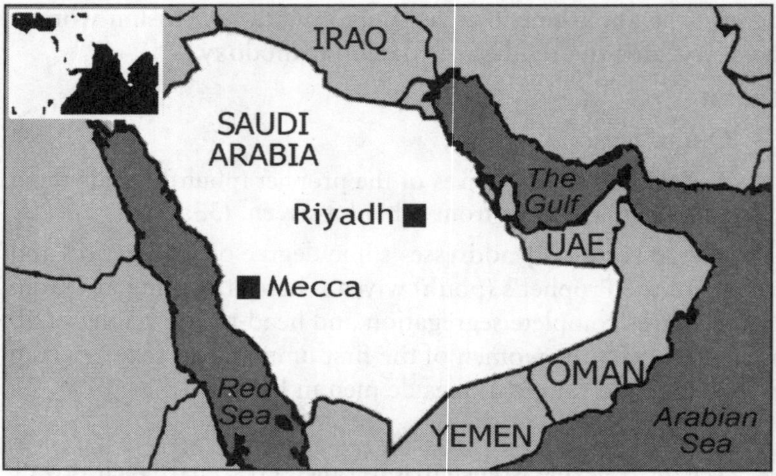

SCHOOLGIRLS DIE IN MECCA STAMPEDE
(MAP: COURTESY OF BBC NEWS)

BBC News

Another defender of Hijab, Sheikh Abul Hosein, a former ambassador and currently Imam of a New York mosque, has led the Muslims to believe that women without Hijab are more

SAUDI POLICE 'STOPPED' FIRE RESCUE
(PHOTOGRAPH: COURTESY OF BBC NEWS)

susceptible to rape than those with Hijab. He also cites the plight of some 50,000 Muslim women in Kosovo who were raped by Slavic men. Such defense is hogwash. When a rapist is bent on raping a woman, Hijab is not going to protect her, as it is not a weapon system that will deter the rapist. Rape is a horrible outcome of wars, and communal as well as racial riots, and tribal hostilities. Women have been raped in various times in history, during the second world war in Germany, during Vietnam war, during the partition of India when Muslim, Hindu and Sikh women were shamed, during the war in Kosovo, during the occupation of Afghanistan by both Russians and Talibans, and during ethnic cleansing in Rwanda, Darfur, and other parts of the world. An Amnesty International report presents the horrible plight of women in Pakistan, a Muslim country. It states:

> Women and girls in Pakistan continue to be subjected to acts of violence within the community, the home and in the custody of the state. Violations in the form of rape, assault, 'honour killing' and mutilation are amongst many concerns continually highlighted by Amnesty International. Impunity for such abuses persists and women continue to face obstacles when trying to gain justice for violations perpetrated against them. The case of Dr Shazia Khalid continues to demonstrate concerns faced by survivors of violence in Pakistan.

Ironically, the Maududis and the Hoseins of the Muslim world have not come forward to condemn such acts of violence committed by their Muslim brethren. They do not have much to gain from the plight of battered and abused Muslim women. Advocacy of Hijab and segregation, of course, makes them champions in the eyes of their zealots, and keep them fat and happy.

BIRTH CONTROL AND ABORTION

The Roe vs. Wade debate, and the conflict between proponents and opponents of abortion have been in existence for several years in the United States. Opponents of abortion have set fire abortion clinic in my own backyard (Atlanta), and shot physicians. Female infanticide is still practiced in India and

China where a female fetus is aborted when substantiated by ultrasound*, and FMG (Female Genital Mutilation) is still performed in a number of African countries.**

Birth control, using various means, has become a global practice and is legislated in several countries. Various rationale and reasons, wrong or right, have been offered by proponents of abortion and birth control—population explosion and associated poverty, life threatening pregnancy, individual apathy toward having children, illicit pregnancy, teenage pregnancy etc.

Justification for abortion as a medical necessity has been refuted by physicians such as Dr. C. Everett Koop, the former Surgeon General of the United States. In his book titled *Let's Talk**** he writes:

> When a pregnant woman decides that she wants an abortion, she is not deciding anything about her health except in rare circumstances.

He writes further:

> I think that abortion is not primarily a medical issue but has become the largest social and political issue.

Although Quran is silent on contraception and birth control, several Ahadith suggest that for the health of a mother and well-being of the family, contraception and birth control are permitted in Islam. It is the Jewish, and not Islamic, belief that practicing birth control is a minor form of burying a child alive. Abortion after a baby is formed, is permitted only if it has been reliably established that continuation of pregnancy will cause the mother's death.****

Quran says:

> Indeed lost are they who have killed their children. (6:140)

---

* *Islam, Opposing Viewpoints,* Edited by Jennifer A. Hurley, p. 78, published by Greenhaven Press.

** According to a Yahoo report published on November 11, 2004.

*** *Let's Talk* by Dr. C. Everett Koop and Dr. Timothy Johns, pp. 18-19, a Zondervan Publication.

**** *The Lawful and Prohibited in Islam* by Al-Qaradawi, pp. 198-201.

There is no disagreement among Muslim scholars on this issue: life begins upon conception when a fetus occupies its place in a woman's body; this fetus gradually develops into a human being and nine months later comes out as a child; when the fetus is aborted, a child is killed; and the Quranic provision stated above is violated.

Quran says:

> You shall not kill your children for fear of want, for it is We* who provide sustenance for them as well as for you; surely killing them is a great blunder. (17:31)

Dr. Bernard Nathanson, a Jew, a staunch advocate of abortion in his early medical practice, one of the founders of National Abortion Rights Action League in the United States, and the former director of the largest abortion clinic in the world, writes in his book, *The Hand of God***:

> The cost of believing in God is minimal; the consequences of doubt may be significant. I have such heavy moral baggage to drag into the next world that failing to believe would condemn me to an eternity.

Dr. Nathanson's transformation from pro-abortion to pro-life is truly Islamic and I commend him for this miraculous change. It is the duty of every Muslim and non-Muslim to discourage abortion and those who seek advice be reminded of the prohibition imposed by all religions.

DILEMMA OF MUSLIM GIRLS IN THE WEST

Muslim girls, specially the children of Muslim immigrants in the West, must endure the dichotomy of an Islamic atmosphere at home and a totally non-Islamic atmosphere outside. Deep down, these Muslim girls are craving to conform to the standards of the western culture while outwardly they must portray the image of their parents' Islamic way of life. The struggle goes on and eventually Muslim parents lose their daughters to

---

* 'We' implies God (Allah).

** *The Hand of God* by Dr. Bernard N. Nathanson, p. 195, a publication of Regency Publishing of Washington D.C.

non-Muslims when they reach legal age. This clash of cultures begins from early childhood. Muslim parents, in general, are particular about taking their children to Sunday School and other Islamic festivities. But in their struggle to accumulate wealth and lead a prosperous life, they often ignore the importance of inculcating Islamic values at home, and solely rely on the Sunday School teachers to raise them as Muslims. Muslim girls do understand the ritualistic aspects of Islam but are, in most case, deprived of the opportunities of understanding Islam. This lack of understanding is the root cause of future conflicts and diversion from Islam. Majority of Muslim parents are themselves ignorant when it comes to understanding Islam. Their emphasis is more on Hijab as well as segregation and less on Islamic teachings. While the struggle goes on, time continues to slip by, and their adolescent girls grow up to be confused young women. Ironically, parents continue to look upon their grown up daughter as a child, and expect total submission to their wishes. They ignore the fact that their child has a mind of her own; she has the ability to analyze, rationalize, and differentiate religious philosophies; she also has the right to choose her lifestyle and religion when she reaches the legal age; parental pressure, coercion, scolding, isolation, detachment, withdrawal of support, and threat have no effect on the young woman. The climax of this horrible parent-daughter relationship is back biting, baseless gossips to hurt each other, defamation of the family, and fragmentation of the fabric that holds the family together. The question one might ask "What has gone wrong?" What has gone wrong is the LACK OF PROPER ISLAMIC EDUCATION from early childhood.

The sentiments and feelings of a young girl are very well described in an article written by Sana Jilani titled "Mom knows Best or Does she?"* Although Miss Jilani has presented the scenario of an Indian family, it is what is happening in Muslim families as well. Muslim girls are hardly any different from non-Muslim girls; from dressing to socializing, they crave to be

---

* *Khabar Magazine*, May 2004, published in Atlanta, Georgia, USA.

like any one else; and they dream of dating, prom, and walking the malls with friends just like most girls do. Some girls in this process have become victims of male perpetrators who have taken advantage of them and sowed the seed for family dissension. The primary responsibility, however, falls upon parents, who often keep themselves aloof and hope that everything is alright.

Parental involvement during the growing years of a girl, especially that of a mother, cannot be over stated. Preparing a girl for an Ivy League School is great. Ignoring her Islamic education from early childhood will, certainly, result in the debacle that most Muslim families are facing in the United States and elsewhere. This debacle can be prevented through proper time management, definition of priorities, and sacrifice of undue social engagements. Muslim parents have no choice but to minimize their trips to the video movie rental shops, and late night weekend parties. Sure enough, they will miss the delicacies that families prepare and share; granted that they will not be able to enjoy the melodies of their native land; albeit, they will be deprived of an intellectual conversation in their native language; undoubtedly, they will not be able to solve global political crises in one evening; but of course, women will not be able to display their recently acquired flashy garment, expensive jewelry, latest hairdo, and professionally done manicure. The message here is "Muslim parents must come to grips with reality and allocate their time and resources in their children's education, both Islamic and academic. SUNDAY SCHOOL IS NOT THE PANACEA.

CONDUCT OF A MUSLIM WOMAN

(Readers should note that a number of topics discussed below also apply to men)

Although advancement of Muslim women in the Islamic infrastructure is of paramount importance, sadly speaking, some Muslim women, in their zeal to imitate the western culture are portraying an image that is offensive to even a very broad-minded non-Muslim man. Their halter tops, sleeveless blouses, hot pants, tight jeans and belly and bosom exposing Hollywood and Bollywood style outfits simply do not fit into the Islamic concept of modesty. Their definition of this copy cat behavior is liberalism. Matrimonial advertisement by some Muslim women in websites includes photographs in sleeveless outfits and confession of smoking and drinking (alcohol). Such advertisements convey only one message to a Muslim man—stay away from them!

A woman's role in any culture, Islamic or otherwise, is very complex. While a man provides the fuel, the woman is the driver of the family engine. She is a wife, a mother, a teacher, a counselor, a heeler, a coach, an adviser, a protector, an investor, and also a provider as well as a fighter when the need arises. The influence of a woman's conduct is extremely important, not only on her immediate family but on the entire community.

The Quranic provision of a woman's conduct is very simple-modesty in all walks of life.

Quran says:

> Present to them the example of the life of this world so like the water we send down from the skies that mingle with the earth to nourish its vegetation. (18:45)

A woman's conduct is similar to the water from the skies. Proper conduct yields a healthy Islamic community while an improper conduct has the propensity to steer the community in a totally indignant and non-Islamic direction.

A brief outline of what women must refrain from is presented below for theirs as well as the benefit of the Islamic community.

SMOKING

Although Quran and Hadith are silent on this subject, socially and medically smoking is unacceptable. Scholars of Islam are unanimous on the ban of Khamr which includes most drugs and tobacco*.

DRINKING (ALCOHOL)

Alcohol consumption is prohibited for all Muslims men and women alike.

---

* Dr. Al-Qaradawi's book, *The Lawful and Prohibited in Islam.*

Quran says:

O believers! Intoxicants and gambling, dedication to stones (idol worshipping) and division by arrows (lottery) are the filthy works of shaitan (devil). Get away from them so you may prosper. (5:90)

DATING AND COMPANIONSHIP

The western concept of dating and living together without marriage are totally forbidden in Islam. While the western culture tolerates pre-marital sex, union of homosexual and bisexual individuals, partner sharing, and extramarital affairs, Islam, as in Christianity, Judaism, and other religions, detests such practices. Although Muslim women in the West are shielded from Islamic punishment for adultery, they are being punished in other ways. Sexually transmitted diseases, incompatible partners, meal ticket searching men who are ready to devour their assets, and divorce are some of the evils that have been inflicted upon them as a result of their zeal to imitate the behaviors of a misguided western woman. Quran has provided guidance to such women at several places as noted below:

1. O believers! Do not be like unbelievers. (3:156)
2. O believers! If you yield to unbelievers they will drag you back to unbelief and you will become the losers. (3:149)
3. Chastity of a woman is emphasized in Quran. Addressing men Quran says:

   Lawful for you is marriage with chaste believing women and also chaste women among the people who were given the book (Christians and Jews) neither committing fornication nor taking them as mistress. (5:5)
4. Guard yourselves against temptation. (8:25)
5. Indeed virtues remove evils. This is a reminder for the mindful. (11:114)
6. Prayer of Joseph (Yusuf) faced with seduction or imprisonment:

   O my Rabb (Lord)! I would rather go to prison than to which (seduction) they invite me, I may, in my youthful folly, feel inclined towards them and become one of the ignorant. (12:33)

7. You shall not commit adultery, surely it is a shameful deed and an evil way (opening the door to other evils). (17:32)
8. Indeed successful are those believers—who guard their private parts. (23:5)
9. However, those who go beyond in that lust are the ones who shall be transgressors. (23:7)
10. Believing Muslim women are forbidden from marrying an adulterer.

    Quran says:

    The fornicator shall not marry any but a fornicatoress or a Mushrik, and like-wise to a fornicatoress, none shall marry her but a fornicator or a Mushrik: such marriages are forbidden to the believers. (24:3)
11. And let those who do not find means to marry keep themselves chaste until Allah enriches them out of his bounty. (24:33)
12. As for the unbelievers, their deeds will disappear like a mirage in a sandy desert. (24:39)
13. Do not be deceived by the free movement of the unbelievers in this land (world). (3:196)
14. Their (unbelievers) enjoyment is brief. Their ultimate house shall be Hell, an evil refuge. (3:197)
15. O believers! Do not follow the footsteps of shaitan (the devil) because anyone who follows the footsteps of shaitan is seduced by him to commit acts of indecency and wickedness. (24:21)

The recent event of same sex marriages in San Francisco, and elsewhere, has let out some women who profess to be lesbian Muslims. Such sexual perversion is totally forbidden in Islam, be that practiced by a man or a woman. It is a major sin. The destruction of the people of Prophet Lut (Lot)(pbuh) who were engaged in homosexuality is very well described in Quran (26:160-175). When Prophet Lut's (pbuh) people refused to abandon this horrible practice, Allah destroyed them with a rain of brimstones.

SPENDING

As shown earlier, women do have the right to spend from their earnings. The two income family concept in the United States and elsewhere, however, puts a burden on a woman to

THE LIFE OF RICH AND FAMOUS

contribute towards the family budget. It becomes a necessity for some families, especially those who are striving to provide expensive private schooling to their children, to depend on the woman's income. Some women, in spite of limited family income, continue to spend their wealth extravagantly as if there is no tomorrow. This overspending culminates from their highly competitive nature. With their wardrobe, home furnishings, elegant mortgaged homes, financed luxury automobiles, charged designer cosmetics, expensive jewelry, vacations, and weekly parties, they have surrounded themselves in a sociological and financial upheaval. The wrath of this lavishness falls on men who can hardly cope up with their spouses' desire to live the life of rich and famous.

THE BOUNTY OF AMERICAN EXPRESS

If Muslim women (and men) today could only study the lifestyle of the Prophet (pbuh), their materialistic attitude would be replaced with a zeal to excel in spiritual fulfilment.

Quran says:

> Allah does not like those who spend their wealth to show off to the people. (4:38)
>
> Wealth and children are an attraction of this worldly life; yet honorable deeds that last forever are better rewarded by your Rabb (God) and hold for you a better hope of salvation. (18:46)
>
> Shall I tell you whose labor will be wasted? Theirs whose effort is misspent in pursuit of pleasures of the world. (18:103,104)

SOCIAL BEHAVIOUR

Very bluntly said, a great number of Muslim women have not been trained to exercise social judgment in mixed public gatherings be that in a mosque, in a private home, or elsewhere. Their desire to socialize only with other women from their region who speak the same language takes precedence over the sentiments and needs of other women who feel isolated and humiliated. A lack of interaction leaves a vacuum which is hard to fill. Ethnicity, arrogance, and negative competitiveness have clouded their minds so badly that they have lost track of their Islamic conduct.

Quran offers a reminder to such women.

Quran says:

> Allah does not love those who are arrogant and boastful. (4:36)
>
> Do not envy that Allah has given some of you more than the others. Men will be rewarded according to their deeds and women will be rewarded according to theirs. (4:32)
>
> Those who desire the life of this world and its splendors, they are given full reward of their deeds therein and shall not be diminished. (11:15)
>
> They are the ones who will have nothing in the hereafter except hellfire. There they shall come to know that their deeds were fruitless and their actions were worthless. (11:16)

In their desire to imitate the western women, some social status conscious Muslim women think nothing of serving alcohol in their parties, attend upper class events in Hollywood style breast exposing attires, and frequent local bars and clubs where they drink and dance with strange men. Yet they call themselves Muslims. Muhammad's (pbuh) soul must be aching to witness these practices of Muslim women. Women's advancement is important, but Islam, on one hand does not condone the extremist view of Purdah and Burqa, and, on the other hand, the liberalism of a western woman. It is neither my intent nor my desire to condemn such women. Quran has provided guidance for them. It is up to them to accept or reject this guidance.

When it comes to interaction with men be that in their profession or in social, religious, and political gatherings, Quran has a specified code of behavior.

Quran says:

> Enjoin the believing women to lower their gaze and guard their modesty; not to display their beauty and ornaments except what normally appears thereof. (24:31)

DRESSING

Dr. Yusuf Al-Qaradawi in his book, *The Lawful and the Prohibited in Islam*, has very well summarized the Islamic code of dressing for women. The essence of this code is the following Hadith:

> Among the dwellers of hell are such women as are clothed yet naked, seduced and being seduced. These (women) shall not enter the Garden (paradise), nor shall its fragrance reach them.

The impetus on the Islamic code of dressing is to avoid imitating non-Muslim women who thrive on attracting men by wearing curve exposing designer clothes and expensive perfume. In the pursuit to find a husband, a western woman has been given the liberty to use any and all means most of which are contrary to the provisions of Quran and the Ahadith.

CRISIS MANAGEMENT

In our fast moving world, crises evolve from both controllable and uncontrollable circumstances. Crises from controllable circumstances culminate due to neglect, carelessness, miscalculations and lack of in-depth analysis of events. Crises from uncontrollable circumstance often include acts of nature, politics, war, terrorism, insurgency, and riots. Without fully understanding the root cause of these circumstances, one is led away with emotion and rationalization only to seek instant remedies, which do not provide meaningful results. Muslim women (and men) can manage these crises by simply reading the Quran as well as Ahadith, and applying the pertinent provisions in their daily life. The following verses from Quran reveal the strength of Quran in this arena:

Quran says:

> O believers! Be patient, excel in patience during confrontation, hold yourselves ready for battle (struggle) and have fear of Allah so that you may succeed. (3:200)

Should you have a dispute in anything, refer it to Allah and His Rasool if you truly believe in Allah and the last day (the Day of Judgment). This course of action will be better and more suitable. (4:59)

Note: The connotation of Allah and Rasool here simply means that one should attempt to resolve a crisis in accordance with the provisions in Quran and Hadith. Litigation and lawsuit must be avoided unless absolutely necessary.

And be patient; verily Allah wastes not the reward of the good doers. (11:15)

Only those who are patient shall receive their reward in full. (39:10)

And verily, whosoever shows patience and forgives; that would truly be from the things recommended by Allah. (42:43)

RESPONSIBILITY TO HER FAMILY

Both Quran and Ahadith have delineated a specific code of conduct for women when it comes to interaction and responsibilities towards the family. Highlights are presented below emphasizing that only the most important entities have been discussed here.

FAVORITISM

A Hadith of the Prophet (pbuh) has stressed equal treatment of all children. Exhibition of undue affection for one and disgust for others is not an Islamic conduct.

LOYALTY

Obedience to Allah and one's husband is stated in Quran. An integral part of this loyalty is to protect the husband's property and make no attempt to transfer or consume his share without his consent.

Quran says:

The righteous women are devoutly obedient (to Allah and their husband) and guard husband's property and their chastity (in his absence). (4:34)

O believers! Do not consume one another's wealth through unlawful means; except it be a trade amongst you by mutual consent. (4:29)

RESPONSIBILTY TO HER PARENTS

Quran has summarized a Muslim's responsibility towards parents in one sentence.

> Be good to your parents. (4:36)

The depth of these five words is extremely hard to understand. It has become a fashion today to celebrate parents' birthdays, mother's day, and father's day. Beyond that, most modern Muslim women (and men) neither allocate their time nor their financial resources for the well-being of their aging parents. In some cases, it is justifiable where a young Muslim family with small children is struggling to make two ends meet and cannot do enough for their parents. Nevertheless, a large number of highly successful and prosperous Muslims (both women and men) have simply abandoned their parents as they do not conform to the elitist lifestyle of their children. These elites have concealed their responsibilities behind the veil of their parents' simplistic lifestyle and the so-called backwardness. This blindness, caused by the shroud of worldly glitter, will end on the Day of Judgment when they will face Allah and account for their deeds.

BEAUTIFICATION AND MAKE-UP

Beautifying to alter the physical condition by plastic surgery is forbidden in Islam. Shaitan (Satan) challenges Allah in Quran and Allah provides guidance to believing women.

> I will create in them false desires. I will order them to tamper with Allah's creation. (4:119) (Satan's challenge)

> The home of such people who follow him (Satan) will be hell, from where they will find no way to escape. (4:121) (Allah's Guidance)

Although in today's business and professional climate, a pleasant appearance is a requirement, any attempt to attract men by excessive makeup and jingling of jewelry is forbidden in Islam.

Quran says:

> Enjoin the believing women—not to display their beauty and ornaments—not to strike their feet in order to draw attention to their hidden trinkets. (24:30, 31)

Marriage in Islam

6

INTRODUCTION

Critics of Islam have been quick to denounce the Islamic provisions of polygamy and divorce. The most common fallacy, that western theologians, televangelist, talk show hosts, and historians have presented to their readers, is the concept of four wives and instant divorce. Hollywood has also contributed in this grossly misunderstood, misrepresented, and misconstrued subject. A part of the blame also lies on Middle Eastern Muslim aristocracy which has provided fuel to opponents of Islam. Their irrational polygamist lifestyle has simply created an aura of irresponsible marital and sexual behavior. In their defense, they have exemplified the practice of polygamy in certain western communities. They feel good about condemning western men who engage themselves in extramarital affairs. Muslims must, however, realize that neither western men nor western communities are on trial. What is on trial is Islam. It becomes, thus, my duty to let my readers know the provisions of monogamy, polygamy, and divorce as prescribed in the Quran and the Ahadith.

THE INSTITUTION OF MARRIAGE

The Prophet (pbuh), recognizing the need for sexual fulfilment of men and women, advocated the institution of marriage between a believing man and a believing woman. He had the wisdom to discourage the catholic concept of monasticism and celibacy. He knew that a religious restriction to suppress the sexual desires of men and women would lead to a cataclysmic diversion from piety, and promote pervasive practices such as Homosexuality, Lesbianism, and Child

Molestation. According to a recent CNN broadcast, the Catholic Church has spent several million dollars to settle child molestation charges by priests.

In one Hadith the Prophet (pbuh) is said to have told his followers:

> I am the one who fears Allah the most among you, yet I fast and I break my fast, I pray and I sleep, and I marry women. He who turns away from my Sunnah has nothing to do with me. (reported by Al-Bukhari)

In another Hadith, reported by both Muslim and Al-Bukhari, the Prophet (pbuh) objected trial to one of his followers (Uthman-ibn-Mazum) living in celibacy.

In a third Hadith, the Allah's Messenger (pbuh) addressing young men said:

> Young men! Those of you who can support a wife should marry as it keeps you from looking at women and preserves your chastity. (reported by Al-Bukhari)

In a fourth Hadith, the Prophet (pbuh) is said to have told his followers:

> The one who marries out of the desire to live a chaste life has the right to the help of Allah.

The above Ahadith solidify the importance of marriage in Islam. This is further stressed in Quran.

Quran says:

> Get the singles among you married as well as those who are fit for marriage among your male slaves and female slaves. (24:32)

The union of a man and a woman, advocated centuries ago by the Prophet (pbuh), a man who could not even read or write, has been solidified by the American voters who have rejected same sex marriages in the election of 2004.

ACCEPTABLE AND PROHIBITED MARRIAGES

ACCEPTABLE

- Marriage with a widow. (Quran 2:234, 4:3)
- Marriage with up to four women (polygamy). (Quran 4:3)

- Marriage with a step-daughter when the husband and wife are divorced and had no sex. (Quran 4:23)
- Marriage with a Muslim woman or a Muslim slave girl. (Quran 4:25, 5:5)
- Marriage of a Muslim man with a chaste Christian or a chaste Jewish woman. (Quran 5:5)

PROHIBITED

- Marriage with a widow with children if the man fears that he cannot be fair with the orphans. (Quran 4:3)
- Polygamy if a man fears that he will not be able to maintain justice between his wives (treat his wives equally). (Quran 4:3)
- Marriage with close relatives. (Quran 4:22, 23, 24, and Hadith)
- Marriage with an adulteress or an adulterer. (Quran 24:3)
- Marriage with a Mushrik (an atheist, an agnostic, a polytheist) (Quran 2:221 and a Hadith)
- Marriage of a Muslim woman with a non-Muslim man. (Quran 2:221, 60:10)
- Marriage with a widow or divorced woman during Iddah (waiting period). (Quran 2:228, 2:234)
- Marriage proposal to a betrothed woman. (Hadith)
- Temporary marriage (Mutah). (Hadith)

JUSTIFICATIONS FOR ACCEPTABLE AND PROHIBITED MARRIAGES

Marriage with a Widow: Prevents a Muslim woman from becoming destitute and a Muslim man gets a companion.

The prohibition in Quran against marrying women with children when a man feels that he cannot be fair with them has a logical reason. It has been seen often that children, Muslim or non-Muslim, fail to establish a bond with their newly acquired step-parent and *vice versa*. This lack of bond results in frequent conflicts. Families spend more time solving petty quarrels and less on their well-being and Islamic duties. It has also led to drug addiction, alcoholism, illicit sexual relations, child molestations, juvenile delinquencies, forced boot-camp or boarding school residency, and frequent 911 calls. Entering into a relationship with a widow (man or a woman) with children is, certainly, a noble act but it must be exercised with caution and a lot of soul searching.

Polygamy: Dr. Yusuf Al-Qaradawi writes*:

> Islam permits Muslims to marry more than one woman in order to resolve some very pressing human problems, individual as well as social.

In pre-Islam Arabia, it was a common practice to have many wives. The Prophet (pbuh) eliminated this practice, and ordered his followers to have no more than four wives. According to Ahadith, men were asked to keep four wives, and divorce the rest. Although there is no documentation as to the plight of the divorced women, logic says that the Messenger (pbuh) of Allah must have asked men to provide for the divorced women in accordance with the Quranic provisions.

The Prophet (pbuh), himself, had nine wives (eleven as per other historians) none of whom was divorced. WAS IT A DOUBLE STANDARD OR A COVER UP UNDER DIVINE DOCTRINE? The logical reason for this deviation was the well-being of the Muslim ummah. While an individual follower of Islam was responsible for his own needs and desires, the Prophet (pbuh) was responsible for all Muslims. Some of his marriages were political in nature. These marriages had united the warring tribes under the umbrella of Islam. Divorcing his wives would hinder the process of DAWA (propagation of the message of Islam) and, most likely, rip the Muslim ummah apart. IT WAS THE PROPHET'S (pbuh) STATESMANSHIP WHICH PREVENTED HIM FROM DIVORCING FIVE (OR SEVEN) OF HIS WIVES.

Both Quran and Hadith have imposed conditions for polygamy.

---

* *The Lawful and Prohibited in Islam,* p. 190.

Quran says:

> Marry women of your choice; two, three, or four; but if you fear that you will not be able to maintain Justice between your wives, then marry only one...so that you may not deviate from the right way. (4:3)

Hadith

The Prophet (pbuh) is said to have told his followers:

> Anyone who does not treat his wives equally will come on the Day of Judgment dragging one part of his body which will be hanging down.*

Based on the provisions of Quran and Ahadith, the Islamic view on this subject is:

> Polygamy in Islam today, is nothing more than a façade which has provided Islam bashers and abusers alike, one more reason to destroy Islam's credibility. Muslim scholars have belabored in explaining the sociological, psychological, medical, and behavioral reasons for polygamy. The bottom line is that Muslims of our time have enough problem coping up with one

THE POLYGAMIST MORMON
(5 wives and 26+ children)
(COURTESY: *TIME MAGAZINE*)

---

* *The Lawful and Prohibited in Islam*, p. 191.

wife, leave alone four. The message to Islam bashers is: "No Muslim in his right mind can satisfy the Quranic provisions of polygamy; if you derive pleasure from bashing, pick on the Mormons and other Polygamists and leave the Muslims alone!"

Marriage with Close Relatives: Marriage is enjoining of two individuals, a man and a woman which includes sexual activities and reproduction of a child. Any society that permits the premises of a family dwelling to become a playground for irrational and pervasive sexual behavior, is bound to ignore the respect, honor, and the bond that exist among family members. It would encourage animal like behavior causing a total breakdown of the family structure and departure from Dawa. Furthermore, communities such as the Parsis of India, which have allowed such marriages, have experienced greater incidences of cancer and other ailments. The Prophet (pbuh), although was neither a social scientist nor a physician, had the ingenuity to prohibit such marriages over fourteen hundred years ago.

Marriage with a Free Muslim Woman or a Muslim Slave Girl: This subject hardly needs any justification. Slavery is no longer in existence. As discussed in Chapter 5, women are breeders of the future generations, and only a believing and practicing woman is capable of raising a child with the same values. Only then the true message of Islam can be spread globally, and reduce anti-Islamic sentiments that is tarnishing the image of Islam, and welfare of Muslims.

Marriage with an Adulterer or Adulteress: In the Islamic perspective, adultery is pre-marital, as well as, extramarital sexual affairs practiced by both men and women. Muslims have been forbidden to marry such men and women, be that a bachelor, a divorcee or a widow. Similar restrictions exist in all major religions. In their zeal to cope up with the western culture, young Muslim men and women, today, fly off to vacation in clandestine destinations prior to marriage under the pretense of "get to know one another". Such free movement poses many questions, the most important being "do they sleep in separate rooms and avoid sexual activities".

The answer herein is left to the reader's imagination. As for Islam, it is an act of adultery and must be avoided.

One of the common problems among Muslim communities today is erroneous blame and rush to judgment when it involves a woman. Hardly anyone questions the chastity or virginity of a man. This is nothing more than male bigotry, and baseless female defamation. Frequently, females are labeled as adulteress whether or not their guilt has been proven according to the Quranic provision of four witnesses, as discussed earlier. When a Muslim man engages in a sexual orgy in the brothels of India, Turkey, Las Vegas, and elsewhere, his piety remains intact while a young Muslim girl's love letter to a young boy is classified as a "SIN". Is this a double standard? Damn right, it is!

Some Muslim scholars have interpreted the word "fornicatoress" in Quran as "prostitute" which is highly debatable. Whether a Muslim woman or a man engages in adultery for money or pleasure does not matter. What matters is their behavioral attitude which destroys the institution of marriage, and the sanctity of male/female relationship, as prescribed in the Quran and the Ahadith. The outcome of such behavior is fragmented family structure, and doubtful lineage of off-springs. There are many children in the United States and elsewhere who do not know "who their father is". In a recent Census Bureau report broadcast by CNN, 35 per cent of children born in the United States are from unwed mothers.

Unfortunately, the multiple partner concept of the West is slowly creeping into the Eastern culture, only to cause social and medical nightmares. Muslims are as vulnerable as non-Muslims.

In *Let's Talk,* Dr. C. Edward Koop writes:

> I disapprove strongly the forms of behavior responsible for most AIDS transmission: promiscuity, homosexual behavior, sex outside marriage, and drug use.

It would be wise for Muslim men and women to look at the horrible plight of western and African men and women whose sexual practices have inflicted upon them various sexually transmitted diseases. I am sure that a large number of Muslim men and women in India, and abroad, have seen the recent Indian movie PHIR MILENGE (We will meet again) in which their hero Salman Khan dies of AIDS, and leaves behind a HIV positive girl friend who fights for survival. Are Muslim men and women ready to face the fate of Salman Khan? Only they can answer this question. PlanetOut.com has listed a number of movies on the same subject, and could be educational for concerned readers (parental discretion is advised).

The World Health Organization (WHO), the Center for Disease Control (CDC) in USA, and concerned celebrities, as well as, physicians around the globe, are doing their best to educate the masses to slow down the spread of AIDS in the twenty-first century.

The Prophet (pbuh), an illiterate Arab, had the wisdom to prohibit adultery, and marriage with an adulterer or an adulteress, centuries ago.

Marriage of a Muslim Woman with a Non-Muslim Man: Muslim women of the twenty-first century, specially those living in a non-Muslim country, have routinely questioned the prohibition of marriage with a non-Muslim man. Some Muslim women have been utterly rebellious, and married non-Muslim men against the Islamic provisions, as well as against the wishes of their families. Such marriages have both social and religious ramifications.

The Islamic concept of marriage is not only enjoining a man and a woman together but also to foster deeper relationship and compassion among the families. If one visualizes this concept in a global perspective, it becomes obvious that both Muslim and non-Muslim communities benefits from the harmony of same faith marriages. The Prophet's (pbuh) marriages had united the warring tribes, who in retrospect, were instrumental in spreading the message of Islam (Dawa). Victory and success depend on unity, be that at a family, community, or national level. A dissimilar faith based marriage satisfies a selfish personal agenda. It has no commitment for the well-being of the family, the community, or children who are often confused and misguided.

While a Muslim man respects the divinity of Christianity and Judaism, and does not force his Christian or Jewish wife to become a Muslim, most Christians and Jews have never accepted the divinity of Islam and the prophethood of Muhammad (pbuh). Their lack of respect for Islam, the Prophet (pbuh), and the Quran has caused numerous wars, and conflicts that are well documented in history. Christian missionaries have devoted their entire life in converting others to Christianity. *"SALVATION IN CONVERSION"* is the belief of every Christian. It is a pity that that Muslim women cannot or do not want to see through this jargon, and get out of such relationship. Their slogans—*Muslim men are JINX, Muslim men are GROSS, Muslim men are BACKWARD,* "I have issues with Islam" etc. are nothing more than defense mechanisms that they are using to justify their non-Islamic relationship. May Allah the Almighty bless both Muslim and non-Muslim women with wisdom, courage, and ability to analyze their relationship!

The following verses from Quran should be sufficient to liberate a confused Muslim woman who has been trapped by an unbeliever, be that a mythical god worshipper, an atheist, or anyone else.

Quran says:

> And do not marry al-Mushrikat till they believe (worship Allah alone). And indeed a believing slave woman is better than a Mushrikah even though she pleases you. And give not (your daughters) in marriage to al-Mushrikun till they believe and verily a believing slave is better than a Mushrik even though he pleases you. Those al-Mushrikun invite you to fire but Allah invite (you) to paradise. (2:221)

> They (believing women) are not lawful (wives) for the disbelievers nor are the disbelievers lawful (husbands) for them (believing women). (2:221)

Marriage with a Christian or Jewish Woman: Inter-religious marriage of a Muslim man with the People of the Book (Christians and Jews) is permitted by Quran.

Quran says:

> And marriage with chaste free believing women and also chaste women among the People who were given the Book before you is made lawful for you. (5:5)

The above provision in Islam is based on the divine nature of Christianity and Judaism. It also depicts the broad mindedness and tolerance of Islam in this area. A Christian or Jewish woman who marries a Muslim man is not required to convert to Islam. She can continue to practice her own faith.

Scholars of Islam, nevertheless, have advised Muslim men to exercise caution and, in order of preference, give a believing Muslim woman precedence over a non-Muslim woman. This advice does make sense for both Muslims and non-Muslims. In our fast moving space age society, men, Muslims or non-Muslims, are already bogged down with daily crises that they must resolve. Any additional religion based bickering between a husband and a wife is like adding fuel to the fire which destroys the relationship, and eventually causes a breakdown of the family.

Mistreatment of Catholic women by Muslim men and their relatives, specially in cases when migrant Muslim men have returned to their native countries, has been reported by the Catholic Church*. These women have been advised by their Church to avoid marrying Muslim men.

This admonishment is another example of the negative aspects of inter-religious marriages, and does make a lot of sense. It sends a message to both Muslims and non-Muslims: *MARRY WITHIN YOUR OWN FAITH.*

Readers who have seen the Hollywood movie, NOT WITHOUT MY DAUGHTER, can appreciate the adversities of an inter-religious marriage. This movie portrays the same exact scenario about which the Catholic church is concerned. The outcome of inter-religious marriages, as portrayed in several Bollywood movies, is not always glamorous, a reality that both Muslims and non-Muslims need to be aware.

Marriage Proposal to a Woman in Iddah (waiting period): A divorced or widowed woman is required to wait for a specified period of time before she can marry another man. In case of a divorced woman, the waiting time is three menstrual periods. This is to assure: (A) *the woman is not pregnant*, and

---

* Published by Yahoo in the Internet on May 14, 2004.

(B) *she may reconcile and go back to her husband complying with the Islamic provision of reunification.*

In case of a widowed woman, the waiting period is four months and ten days. This waiting period provides a woman time to: (A) *relieve her sorrow,* (B) *assess her future needs and desires,* and (C) *ascertain if she is pregnant.*

In either case (divorced or widowed), the waiting period is regarded as a part of the previous marriage. A marriage during this period is regarded as polygamy which is not permitted in Islam for Muslim women.

Marriage Proposal to a Betrothed Woman: Betrothal, in literal sense, is a contract for future marriage. When a Muslim man proposes to a Muslim woman, it constitutes a contract even though not legal. A proposal by another Muslim man is synonymous to a bidding war which Islam dislikes. Dr. Al-Qaradawi has mentioned two Ahadith to reinforce this prohibition. The Prophet is said to have told his followers:

> A Believer is a brother to another Believer. It is, therefore, not lawful for him to outbid his brother in buying something or to propose to a woman when his brother has done so unless he gives him permission. (reported by Muslim)
>
> A man must not propose to another man's betrothed woman unless he withdraws or gives him permission. (reported by Al-Bukhari)

The evils of a love-triangle has been portrayed in both Hollywood and Bollywood movies, the most recent one being CLOSER. This prohibition in Islam cures one more social ailment of our time, and curtails violence among Muslims.

Temporary Marriage (Mut'a or Mutah): The concept of Mut'a was introduced by the Prophet (pbuh) during the infancy of Islam when the entire Islamic jurisprudence was going through a revolutionary transition from ignorance to enlightenment. The logical reason for Mut'a was to curb sexual improprieties among Muslim men whose prolonged engagements, because of war or other duties, would not fulfil their sexual needs.

The Quranic justification for Mut'a stems from the following verse:

Quran says:

> All women—are lawful provided you seek them in marriage with gifts from your property (dowry), desiring Chastity and no lust. Give them their dowry as an obligation. For the benefit you received from your marriage relationship. However, there is no blame on you if you change your agreement of dowry with mutual consent. (4:24)

Mut'a, which was initiated and terminated in accordance with the Islamic practice, was a contract marriage. The woman was paid her Mehr (dowry) and additional funds upon termination. Children born from Mut'a were supported by the man.

Although verse 4:24 is not specific about temporary marriage, explanations offered by various scholars have led Muslims to believe that the principal thrust of this verse was to allow Mut'a which was prevalent in the Prophet's time in Medina. While verse 4:24 has not been abrogated, and there is no Hadith that prohibits Mut'a, Sunni Muslims tend to believe that the Prophet (pbuh) had prohibited this practice in his lifetime. Shia Muslims have taken exception to this belief, and postulated that Umar, the third Caliph, imposed a Prohibiton against this practice. Unfortunately, even today, Muslims are taking undue advantage of this provision. An article published in the Indian newspaper, *The Telegraph*, on December 5, 2004, states:

> More and more sex workers in Pakistan are practicing "mutah" to gain a sense of legitimacy and beat the law of the land. Mutah marriages are not limited to Pakistan. In India's Hyderabad, such incidents are common when cash-rich Arab Sheikhs come searching for young brides. In most cases, the marriages last a night or so and greedy clerics even issue marriage/divorce certificates to provide legal cover. Poverty, ignorance and lust seem to be paving the way for exploitation of women, on both sides of the border.

For further information on this subject, the readers are advised to consult shiachat.com, telegraphindia.com, and other websites.

PRE-MARITAL FREEDOM ALLOWED IN ISLAM

Both Muslims and non-Muslims have presented a rigid picture of Islam when it comes to pre-marital activities of Muslim men and women. While Islam does not permit pre-marital sex, frequent unsupervised dating prior to marriage, and other practices prevalent in the Western culture, it (Islam) does allow some degree of freedom in matters of matrimony as summarized below:

- Both men and women have the freedom to choose their future spouse so long as they are believing and practicing Muslims. Men are permitted to marry chaste Christian or Jewish women.
- Muslim men and women are permitted to see and evaluate their future mates in accordance with a Hadith of the Prophet (pbuh) reported by Al-Bukhari.
- Muslim men and women are allowed to have a limited number of outings so as long as an adult chaperon goes with them, and these outings do not include non-Islamic activities.
- A father or a guardian, according to a Hadith, cannot force a girl to select a particular man for marriage as seen among Muslims all over the world. The girl has the right to accept or reject a man proposed by her father or guardian. Nevertheless, in the selection process, a girl should consider her own welfare, as well as the welfare of the family, and the community.

Divorce in Islam

7

INTRODUCTION

Divorce is a curse which is not only disliked by Islam but by Christianity, Judaism, and other religions as well. While the frequency of divorce among Muslims has not reached the western proportion, it is escalating rapidly only to cause destruction of the family and the community.

In strict Islamic perspective, the process of divorce begins from a lack of understanding of individual responsibilities of a man and a woman as prescribed in the Quran and the Ahadith. The frequent bickering, yelling, shoving, beating, use of profanity, distrust, accusation, and a slew of malicious behavior patterns that husbands and wives depict as a precursor to divorce, are the results of their departure from an Islamic way of life. For the benefit of both Muslim and non-Muslim readers, therefore, it would be wise to examine Islamic guidelines which foster love, affection, compassion, understanding, trust, obedience, and other virtues that are vital for a couple to live in peace and avoid a walk on the path of divorce. An insight into the injunctions of the Quran and the Ahadith will, no doubt, diffuse the daily tension and create an environment of peaceful co-existence.

QURANIC INJUNCTIONS

Quran says:

O you who believe! Seek help in patience and as-salat (prayers). Truly Allah is with As-Sabirin (the patients). (2:153)

Who when afflicted with calamity, say "To Allah we belong and truly to Him we shall return. (2:156)

And eat up not one another's property unjustly. (2:188)

Do not use Allah's name in your oath as an excuse to prevent you from dealing justly, guarding against evil, and making peace between people. (2:224)

And women have rights similar to those of men.....
But men have a darajah* over them. (2:228)

Do not entrust your property which Allah has made a means of support for your family, to feeble-minded people for investment in business. (4:5)

Allah accepts only the repentance of those who do evil in ignorance and foolishness, and repent soon afterwards, it is they whom Allah will forgive. (4:17)

O you who believe! You (men) should not treat them (wives) with harshness...treat them with kindness even if you dislike them; it is quite possible that you dislike something in which Allah has placed much good. (4:19)

Men (husbands) are the protectors and maintainers of women (wives)...the righteous women (wives) are devoutly obedient (to Allah and to their husbands) and guard in husband's absence what Allah orders them to guard (*e.g.* their chastity, husband's property). (4:34)

If a woman fears cruelty or desertion from her husband, there is no blame if both of them agree to reconcile by means of a compromise, after all compromise is better. (4:128)

PROVISIONS OF AHADITH

A number of Ahadith of the Prophet (pbuh) describe the codes of conduct to which Muslim men and women (husbands and wives) must adhere to keep their relationship alive and avoid divorce. A summary of these Ahadith is presented below:

- With regard to rights of a wife: The Prophet (pbuh) said. "Feed and clothe her as you feed and clothe yourself; you should never hit her face or put her down; or cut yourself from her.

---

* darajah: degree of responsibility, slight superiority.

- With regard to supporting a wife: The Prophet (pbuh) said, "Wasting the sustenance of his dependents is sufficient sin for a man."
- With regard to curbing the desire to punish: The Prophet (pbuh) said to a servant, "If it were not the fear of retaliation on the Day of Resurrection, I would have beaten (you) with this miswak (stick)."
- With regard to beating of a wife: The Prophet (pbuh) said, "None of you must beat your wife as a slave is beaten, and have intercourse with her at the end of the day."
- About the man who beats his wife: The Prophet (pbuh) said, "Certainly those who beat their wives are not the best among you."

COMPARISON OF DIVORCE IN ISLAM, CHRISTIANITY, AND JUDAISM

Islam and Christianity

Islam	Christianity
• Divorce permitted when all measures have failed. • Permits marriage of divorcees after a specified waiting period. • Prohibits marriage of former spouses unless the wife marries another man who divorces her. • Requires three divorces by a man with waiting period after the first and the second divorce. • Husband must pay the Mehr if it has not been paid to the wife. • Permits a woman to seek divorce through a process called Khula. Wife must return the Mehr if it has been paid.	• Gospel of Jesus prohibits divorce except on grounds of adultery. • Prohibits marriage to divorced men and women. • Marriage of a man to a divorced woman and that of a woman to a divorced man is considered adultery. (Matt 5:31-32) (Mark 10:11-12) • Protestants permit divorce on grounds of adultery, betrayal of husband, and other reasons. • Catholics require men to divorce their unchaste wives.

Islam and Judaism

Islam	Judaism
• Divorce permitted when all measures have failed. • Permits marriage of divorcees after a specified waiting period. • Prohibits marriage of former spouses unless the wife marries another man who divorces her. • Requires three divorces by a man with waiting period after the first and the second divorce. • Husband must pay the Mehr if it has not been paid to the wife. • Permit's a woman to seek divorce through a process called Khula. Wife must return the Mehr if it has been paid.	• Jewish law requires a man to divorce. His wife if found guilty of adultery. • Prohibits marriage of a man to his former wife if she has married another man. • Talmud allows a Jewish man to divorce his wife for no reason. Wife's consent is not needed. • A Jewish man can divorce his wife with a single bill of divorce. • Only a man can initiate a divorce in Judaism. • Ketubah require a man to pay a good amount of money to his wife unless misconduct is the reason for divorce.

A detailed explanation of the provisions of Quran and Ahadith is not necessary. The important aspect to recognize is the depth of the Islamic deterrence against destruction of husband-wife relationship which, ultimately, results in a divorce. Sanctity and permanency of marriage were very dear to the Prophet (pbuh) and history has shown that he did not divorce any of his nine wives. To be fair, he spent equal time with all his wives. He never entered into beating his wives and servants. If only Muslim husbands and wives would follow the Islamic guidelines and the Prophet's (pbuh) approach to solving life's issues, the word divorce will become extinct from the Islamic dictionary.

THE PROCESS OF ISLAMIC DIVORCE

DIVORCE BY A MAN (HUSBAND)

In Islam, a man must divorce his wife three times for the divorce to be final. Nevertheless, there is no such thing as an instant final divorce. Islamic divorce is somewhat different from the Jewish divorce which only requires a Bill of Divorce initiated by the husband and the divorce is done. Within the realm of three divorces in Islam, emphasis on reconciliation has been considered as the Prophet (pbuh) despised divorce and said to his followers:

"Among lawful things, divorce is most hated by Allah."

The pronouncement of three divorces at one time or in one breath is a deviation from the Islamic provisions, and does not constitute an Islamic divorce. A believing Muslim can, certainly, understand the gravity of divorce by simply following the Quran and the Ahadith. The Islamic process of divorce is shown in the following tables:

FIRST DIVORCE

The Process	Requirements
Step # 1	Step # 1
A man divorces his wife by pronouncing it in the name of Allah.	The woman must be clean (not menstruating or having discharge after childbirth); the husband had no sexual Intercourse after menstruation; the woman may or may not be pregnant.
Step # 2	Step # 2
The woman remains in a state of Iddah (waiting period of four months).	The couple must share the same dwelling apart from one another.
Step # 3	Step # 3
The husband and wife reconcile during the Iddah.	The divorce is void and no further action is needed.
Step # 4	Step # 4
The couple reconcile after the expiration of Iddah.	The couple must remarry by performing Nikah to negate the divorce.

SECOND DIVORCE

The Process	Requirements
Step # 1	Step # 1
The man pronounces the divorce.	Restrictions are the same as first divorce.
Step # 2	Step # 2
The woman remains in Iddah.	Same as for the first divorce.
Step # 3	Step # 3
The couple reconcile during Iddah.	The divorce is void.
Step # 4	Step # 4
The couple reconcile after Iddah.	They must remarry as after the first divorce.

THIRD DIVORCE

The Process	Requirements
Step # 1	Step # 1
The man divorces his wife the third time.	Restrictions are as for first and second.
Step # 2	Step # 2
The woman remains in Iddah.	The divorce is final and the couple must separate. The man must pay the Mehr and mutually agree on financial support.
Step # 3	Step # 3
Both are free to marry another person.	A man or a woman cannot remarry his or her former spouse unless another man marries the woman and subsequently divorces her.

DIVORCE BY A WOMAN (KHULA)

When a husband refuses to divorce his wife, and the wife does not want to remain married for valid reasons, she is entitled to initiate a separation process called Khula. An Islamic Judge hears the wife's complaints and, if satisfied, orders the husband to divorce her. If the judge is not satisfied, or the woman does not have a valid reason, her request is denied and she continues to remain married to the man.

Both Quran (2:229) and a Hadith of the Prophet (pbuh) (Al-Bukhari, 5273) dictate this separation procedure. Upon return of the Mehr (dowry), the husband says: *I separate from you OR I let you go.*

Scholars have ruled that when a woman secures a divorce through man-made laws (a court granted divorce), this divorce is invalid unless supplemented by Khula. Without Khula, she continues to remain married and, though regarded as divorced according to court decrees, cannot marry another man.

THE QUANDARY IN ISLAMIC DIVORCE

The process of divorce and its various elements are not always clear cut. For example, if a man takes an oath not to have sexual relationship with his wife, and the elapsed time exceeds four months, scholars of Islam have differed in the final disposition.

A. The man must divorce his wife.
B. The divorce is final without any court (Islamic) judgment.
C. The matter should be turned over to an Islamic court which will decide on the validity or annulment of the divorce.

The quandary in the Islamic provision of four months is from a man's perspective.

Quran says:

> Those who take an oath not to have sexual relations with their wives must wait for four months. If they reconcile and restore their relationship, surely Allah is Forgiving and Merciful. (2:26)

Existing Ahadith also only address a man taking his wife back, or divorcing her after the four-month waiting period.

Jurists and scholars have simply failed to address this subject from a woman's viewpoint. A discussion on a stubborn wife's refusal to conciliate, and rekindle marital, as well as sexual relationship with her willing and conciliatory husband, is nowhere to be found. A reader may, therefore, reach the conclusion that, for all practical purposes, divorce in Islam is a one way street on which the man walks in one direction, a stubborn liberated wife walks in the opposite direction, and a willing non-liberated wife gasps for breath and has no sense of direction.

Dr. Al-Qaradawi has presented the plight of a neglected woman by quoting the following Hadith:

> Umar, the second caliph of Islam, during making a round in Madinah, heard a woman sing:
>
> The night is long, the darkness all around me
> I am sleepless, for I have no friend to play with
> I swear by Allah that had there been no fear of Him
> This cot would be shaking from side to side

This lonely woman's song sends a powerful message to both men and women, Muslims or non-Muslims. It depicts the need for emotional and sexual fulfilment. This fulfilment can either be achieved in the proper Islamic manner or by adultery.

Stubborn men and women who have chosen the destructive course of neglect and divorce, have a lot to learn from this song. "I have no friend to play with" alludes to the fact that both men and women, who are separated or divorced, are mentally and emotionally torn apart to the extent that they are ready to fall in the arms of the first person who shows even an ounce of affection. This culminates the beginning of a relationship, often sexual in nature, and sows the seed for adultery.

The woman in the song is a God-fearing woman, and controlling her urge to be in a cot with another man. But men and women today enjoy enormous amount of freedom. Exposure to sexually explicit material only adds to the already bubbling desire for sexual intercourse and fornication. Escort services and brothels prey on these men and women who have been deprived of sex. The conflict between sexual exhilaration and Islamic doctrines goes on and, guess who loses the doctrines.

Deception and justifications for deception have become the norms of the modern Muslim men and women who deceive none but themselves. The state of the Muslims can be summarized with the following quotation:

> Oh, what a tangled web we weave, when first we practice to deceive.
>
> (Sir Walter Scott, *Marmion*)

DIVORCE OF MIGRANT MUSLIM MEN AND WOMEN

Migrant Muslim men and women living in a country where they do not have access to an Islamic court, have often sought divorce through the legal system of their country of residence. In the United States, it is usually the Superior Court of a county (called Parish In Louisiana) which grants divorces to its residents. Acceptance or rejection of such divorces have been hotly debated by Muslim scholars and researchers. There is no unanimity on this subject. Whether or not the Islamic community accepts the non-Islamic divorce, hardly matters. Aside from keeping the door open for future reconciliation, it achieves nothing that is beneficial for the family. No one wins from court granted divorces except the lawyers. It divides, not only the assets of the family, but also the minds and hearts of family members. Children grow up without a father, his love, and guidance; both husbands and wives lead a lonely life; both incomes suffer a bigger tax bite; and children's academic as well as Islamic education suffers because a single working parent hardly has time for any thing other than putting food on the table. In a nutshell, a divorce granted by a non-Muslim court has all the elements of the legal system of a country but devoid in a lesson on the unity of the family and permanency of the family structure. Muslim men and women must rely on the Islamic deterrence to divorce rather than jumping on the band wagon of superior court judges and clerks.

ISLAMIC DETERRENCE TO DIVORCE

Jurists and scholars of Islam have provided rulings and guidance which strongly support the deterrence of divorce in Islam. The Islamic Sharia (Law) has made divorce unlawful unless all avenues of reconciliation have failed. Some jurists have gone to the extent of declaring it (divorce) Haram (unlawful) as they believe that divorce is injurious to both husband and wife and damages their interest.

Muslim men and women, who have divorced their spouses just to enjoy a variety of sexual pleasures, have been classified by the Prophet (pbuh) as TASTERS. In one Hadith the Messenger (pbuh) of Allah said:

I do not like the tasters men and women
And Allah does not like tasters men and women.

The provision of reconciliation and waiting period between divorces in Quran, serves a deep-rooted purpose *i.e.* continuation and permanency of the union of a man and a woman as well as the institution of marriage that were very dear to the Prophet (pbuh). It is reemphasized here that the Prophet (pbuh) did not divorce any one of his nine wives.

Divorce is permissible only after all efforts of reconciliation have failed. When the rift between two individuals enjoined in matrimony is so colossal that all sentimental values have disappeared, and not even a trace of mutual respect, love, and trust exists. It is in the best interest of the couple to separate in a peaceful manner. Under no circumstances, Islam approves abandoning of children which is being practiced by both Muslim and non-Muslim men and women today. The zeal for revenge has driven men and women to seek court injunctions which either restrict parental visitations or ban parental visitations all together. In an effort to get even with their former husbands, some Muslim women have obtained court orders that have snatched away the father's parental rights. Such victorious women fail to realize that they have paved the way for a fatherless upbringing of their children. The adverse reaction of such upbringing becomes apparent when these children grow up to be any thing but Muslims. Boys often become psychiatrist cases and girls seek father figures in their adulthood hoping to restore years of lost emotional fulfilment. Often times, these girls end up with wrong men who dump them after taking advantage of them. Considering these harsh realities of our time, Muslim men and women need to do a lot of soul searching before considering divorce. Spiritual strength is the best deterrence to divorce. This strength can be acquired only through understanding Islamic values and following an Islamic way of life.

Glossary

Aberration	: Deviation from the truth.
Abode	: Residence, place.
Admonishment	: Advice, the act of counseling against wrong doing.
Admonishment	: Act of advising or warning.
Ahadith	: Plural of Hadith, practices and statements of Muhammad (pbuh).
Anathema	: A curse or denunciation.
Ascension	: A rising, the act of moving up.
Attune	: To tune, to bring into harmony, to adjust.
Aura	: An air.
Benevolent	: Kind, possessing love for mankind.
Canonical	: Pertaining to the rule of a religious order.
Cataclysmic	: Flooding, sweeping.
Clandestine	: Secret, private, hidden from public view.
Cliché	: Stereotype phrase.
Conjectural	: Formation of an opinion based on insufficient evidence.
Connotation	: What constitutes meaning of a word.
Culminate	: Produce, to reach the highest point.
Debilitating	: Weakening, reduced.
Defamation	: Slander, cause injury to reputation.
Defunct	: Dead, lifeless.
Delineate	: To draw the line.

Dichotomy	: Division, cutting in two.
Disgruntled	: Dissatisfied.
Dissension	: A disagreement.
Dogma	: A settled opinion or belief.
Effacement	: To destroy as a figure (implies humbleness, humility).
Emanation	: To flow forth or issue from a source.
Emphatically	: With force of voice of opinion.
Erroneous	: Containing errors or mistakes.
Exemplify	: To show or illustrate by example.
Exponential	: Out of proportion, excessive.
Foe	: An enemy.
Fiqh	: Jurisprudence.
Foster	: To promote, to encourage.
Hijra	: Migration, immigration.
Impetus	: Force, momentum.
Impoverished	: Poor.
Inculcate	: To teach and enforce by repetition.
Indignant	: Disgusted, having no dignity.
Ingenuity	: The power of wisdom and ability.
Intertwined	: To be united by twining or twisting with one another.
Jurisprudence	: Knowledge of the laws, customs.
Khalifa	: Caliph or Calif, religious and political authority given to an individual in Islam.
Madhhab or Mazhab	: Religious philosophy or channel.
Malicious	: Carrying ill will or bad feeling.

Marvel	: A wonder, an object of great astonishment.
Masjid	: Mosque.
Mushrikat	: Disbelieving women.
Mushrikah	: Disbelieving woman.
Mushrikun	: Disbelieving men.
Mushrik	: Disbelieving man.
Mulla or Mullah	: A religious leader, a scholar of Islam.
Omission	: The act of omitting or neglect.
Opulent	: Wealthy, rich.
Perpetrator	: One who is guilty of doing wrong.
Pitfall	: A trap.
Pragmatic	: Practical.
Precursor	: A forerunner, what comes first.
Propensity	: Tendency, inclination.
Pseudomorphous	: Not having the true form.
Puritanism	: The doctrine of superior discipline.
Quandary	: A state of difficulty, perplexity.
Rabb	: Lord, God, Allah.
Reformation	: The act of forming anew.
Renunciation	: The act of renouncing or denying.
Sharia	: Islamic law.
Slew	: Abundance.
Subservience	: Acting as a subordinate, sucking up to someone.
Sunna or Sunnah	: Practices of Muhammad (pbuh).
Tantamount	: Of great significance or value.

Transition	: Change or process of change, passage from one state to another.
Transmigration	: The passing of a soul into another body.
Ummah	: Community, Nation.
Unanimity	: The state of agreeing in opinion.
Vehemently	: With great force.
Zealot	: One who gets carried away.

References

English Translation of the Meaning of *AL-QUR'AN* by Muhammad Farooq-I-Azam Malik, published by The Institute of Islamic Knowledge, Houston, Texas, USA.

THE NOBLE QUR'AN, English Translation of the Meanings and Commentary by Dr. Taqi-ud-Din Al-Hilali and Dr. Muhammad Muhsin Khan published by King Fahd Complex for the Printing of the Holy Qur'an, Medina, Kingdom of Saudi Arabia.

The Translation of the Meaning of *Summarized Sahih Al-Bukhari* by Dr. Muhammad Muhsin Khan, published by Maktaba Dar-us-Salam, Riyadh, Kingdom of Saudi Arabia.

The Decline and Fall of Roman Empire by Edward Gibbons, published by Random House Publishing Group.

Islam, A Short History by Karen Armstrong, published by Random House.

Muhammad in The Bible by Dr. J. Badawi, an e-book, published by IBS in co-operation with www. Al-Sunnah.com.

Man's Religions by John Boyer Noss, published by Macmillan Publishing, New York, USA.

III&E Brochure on ISLAM, published by The Institute of Islamic Information and Education, Chicago, Illinois, USA.

Sufism by Carl W. Ernst, published by Shambhala Publication, Boston, Massachusetts, USA.

Wahabi Islam by Natana J. Delong-Bas, published by Oxford University Press, New York, USA.

Faith and Power, The Politics of Islam by Edward Martimer, a Random House Group Publication.

Islam in the World by Milse Ruthven, published by Oxford Univrsity Press, New York, USA.

Islam, Judaism and Christianity, Theological and Historical Applications by Heribert Busse, published by Marks Wiener Publishers, Princeton, New Jersey, USA.

Hinduism and Buddhism by Coomaraswamy and Ananda Kentish, published by Greenwood Publishing Group, Connecticut, USA.

Buddhism by Kevin Trainer, published by Oxford University Press, New York, USA.

Satanic Verses by Salman Rushdie, a Penguin Group Publication.

The Encyclopedia of Child Abuse by Robin Clark and Judith Clark, published by Facts on File, New York, USA.

The Shade of Swords by M.J. Akbar, a Routledge Group Publication, London.

Pakistan, A Modern History by Ian Talbot, published by St. Martin's Press, New York, USA.

Encyclopedia of Islam by Koninkliijke Brill NV, Leiden, The Netherlands.

Arrogant Capital by Kevin Phillips, published by Little Brown & Co., New York, USA.

Jesus-Prophet of Islam, published by Ta-Ha Publishers Ltd., London, UK.

The Political Language of Islam by Bernard Lewis, published by the University of Chicago Press, USA.

The Lawful and Prohibited in Islam by Dr. Yusuf Al-Qaradawi, an ATP Publication, Burridge, Illinois, USA.

'Article on Islam' by Karen Armstrong, published in the *Time Magazine,* USA Edition on October 1, 2001.

'Women in Islam', a *Time Magazine* article, published by Lisa Beyer in the USA Edition on November 25, 2001.

'Mom Knows Best or Does She?', an article published by Sana Jilani in *The Khabar Magazine,* published in Atlanta, Georgia, USA.

Statistics on Child Abuse, published by Wild Iris Medical Education Program, New York, USA.

'Islam and Women' by Muhammad Asadi, an Internet article published by www.bigissueground.com.

An Associated Press (AP) report, published by Yahoo on November 23, 2004 on 'Child Abuse'.